WALKING IN HIS STEPS

A FORTY-DAY JOURNEY

DR. JOE PETTIGREW

Walking In His Steps

ISBN 9798303929326

Published by *ITZ Publishing*
Copyright © 2024 by Joseph Pettigrew
All rights reserved.

Unless otherwise noted, Scripture notations are from the New International Version (The Holy Bible) copyright 2011 by *Biblica*, an International Bible Society publishing ministry.

Used by permission. All rights reserved.

Printed in the United States of America

PREFACE

Walking In His Steps was created to be relevant and Biblically sound for men and women seeking a closer walk with Jesus Christ. Written as both a small group study and a study for individuals, both have found it to be informative and valuable in their daily walks. The focus is to help you be better resourced to fight the cultural battles for your heart and soul and help you influence your family and friends for Jesus Christ. You will be exposed to practical truths and Biblical principles through the transparency of the 40-day curriculum. In addition, you will relate to how today's material culture is trying to intimidate us into becoming politically correct instead of Biblically obedient.

God considers forty days a spiritually significant period of time. We are creatures of habit, and we often find ourselves in a rut where we do the same things over and over. There are certain areas of our lives where we are willing to get out of our comfort zone, and yet other places we would just as well be left alone. Throughout the Bible, God uses forty days as a significant time period to accomplish His purposes. You will find briefly examined a number of instances in the Bible in which forty days are used. While forty days may not appear magical to you, it seems to be a time frame that God has used several times to change the world.

Instances in the Bible Where God Made Major Changes and Transformations after Forty Days

It rained for forty days and forty nights when God wanted to cleanse the world and start over.
(Genesis 7:12)

Noah waited another forty days after it rained before he opened a window in the ark.
(Genesis 8:6)

Moses was on the mountain with God for forty days—twice.
(Exodus 24:18; 34:28–29)

Moses' face shone after the forty days on the mountain.
(Exodus 34:29)

It took the spies forty days to search out the Promised Land and bring back fruit.
(Numbers 13:25)

Goliath challenged the Israelites for forty days before being killed by David.
1 Samuel 17:16)

Jonah warned the city of Nineveh that they had forty days until God would overthrow the city. The people repented in those forty days, and God spared the city.
(Jonah 3:4, 10)

Jesus fasted for forty days in the wilderness.
(Matthew 4:2)

Satan tries to tempt Jesus for forty days.
(Matthew 4:1–2)

Jesus was seen on Earth for forty days after His resurrection.
(Acts 1:3)

Despite our fast-paced culture and its stressful impact on each of us, ***Walking In His Steps*** will empower you to understand that God's Word is just as applicable today as it was when written! The study is designed to appeal to men and women who have already accepted Jesus as their personal Savior. However, this can be a perfect opportunity for you to invite friends to be exposed to the Word of God through an exciting curriculum. This study is designed by using seven topics, each with a daily reading plan that covers forty days. We pray that you find this study a thought-provoking, Biblically-based curriculum.

TABLE OF CONTENTS

WEEK ONE:

Why Are You Here?

Day 1

You Are Here For A Reason

"Do not be conformed to this world, but be transformed by the renewal of your mind, that by testing you may discern what the will of God is, what is good and acceptable and perfect."
Romans 12:2

DAILY PRAYER

God, I love you. I am so busy. I feel pulled in every direction. Please help me focus on the one thing you call me to do—Bring glory to You. As I go through my day, help me realize everything I do that brings glory to You is my purpose. Show me, Lord, how to bring glory to you in everything I do, and Jesus, please forgive me when I fall short. I love you, Jesus.

Congratulations, you are here for a reason! That reason that only you and Jesus know for sure, but you are here for a reason. No magic bullet is offered here to reveal this to you; however, more and more people ask themselves fundamental questions like: Why did God create me? In addition to finding out these answers, we often find ourselves frustrated, afraid, and confused. The world is changing, and things don't make sense anymore. It often feels as if we live on a merry-go-round, asking when and where can we get off. We know we shouldn't worry, but we need some answers. We wake up, work hard, care for our family, go home, and then go to bed. Tomorrow, we get up and do it all over again. You may have asked yourself, Is this all there is to life? We really do want to know why you are here?

Do you ever feel your life is on autopilot? We are all living in a crazy time, which is one thing that makes this study unique. With everything happening around us, it is easy to forget that God created you with a specific purpose for where you are right now. People travel throughout the world, trying to answer this one crucial question. They attend seminars, read books, go to counseling sessions, and even check out of life to find themselves. Yet, God tells us in Scripture that He has a specific reason for you, a purpose unlike anyone else's.

"For I know the plans I have for you," declares the Lord, "plans to prosper you and not to harm you, plans to give you hope and a future."
Jeremiah 29:11

Looking back, some of the most uncomfortable moments in your life have come when you were asked to do something you had never been asked to do before-something out of your comfort zone. When that happens, we can count on that God is placing us in this situation because He has something He wants us to learn. God has many great ways to prepare us for what He has planned. When preparing to free Israel's people from slavery, He chose Moses to be his leader. Do you remember what Moses said? Are you kidding me, God? I am the wrong one for this. Well, that's not what he said to God, but rather, "Who am I to lead the people of Israel out of Egypt?" Moses had lived in three cultures. He was raised a Jew as a child, was educated by the Egyptians, and grew up among the Midianites. When God asked, Moses questioned his identity and ability. "I'm not very good with words. Please, Send anyone else!" It sounds as if Moses is more like us than we think, he didn't want God to pull him out of his comfort zone either. He had failed once in a big way. He was no longer the prince of Egypt, because he was wanted and accused of murdering a poor shepherd. Moses must have possessed genuine self-doubt about his leadership abilities. It sounds like he was thinking, at my age, this appointment would mess up my retirement plans. He was past his prime and felt unsure that he could do anything worthwhile for people, but God chose Moses. He was a reluctant leader but he stepped up to the challenge. Moses accomplished his purpose not because of his wisdom but because God's power was revealed in His weakness. It took a while, but Moses discovered at an old age why he was placed on this Earth.

Why did God make you? Why did God decide to create you? These questions are as old as the human race itself. Some believe their goal in life is to create wealth and be rich. Some believe they were made to be happy and enjoy their toys. And yet others believe they were put here as part of a plan. Your purpose is to love Jesus and all those around you while becoming the best version of yourself possible. Have you ever met someone who believes there is no purpose to their life but instead just a series of coincidences that happen? You were created for a reason: the clues are in plain view. Your purpose is so deeply embedded in your daily life that it can easily be overlooked.

"But I have raised you for this very purpose, that I might show you my power and that my name might be proclaimed in all the earth."
Exodus 9:16

God placed you in your current job for a reason. God put you within your present family for a reason. God even set you in your church for a reason. Finally, God placed you in this study for a reason. Jesus has been present and active in your life since the very beginning. He created you to bring glory to Him in everything you do, so the real question is, how do you determine His will for your life?

It often seems that everyone, except us, seems to know why we were placed on this Earth. Sure, you have a gut feeling; however, there is always a tiny voice in the back of your mind asking, How do you know if you are following God's plan? Growing up, you surely remember having a friend who seemed to understand their reason for being here. Some were destined to be school teachers, cowboys, policemen, nurses, or princesses. Once we reached high school, those plans changed to be accountants, attorneys, NFL stars, or physicians. Some of them ended up doing what they originally thought, but not many. However, most had no idea why God put them here in elementary, high school, or college. If we are honest, some of us are still trying to figure it out. We go to school, graduate, find our soul mate, and begin having children. Soon after the bills start pouring in and our responsibilities increase. Whatever job we start out doing often becomes our life's work. We didn't necessarily choose our occupation; it chose us. At the beginning we weren't looking for our life's calling that would showcase why God placed us here. We were looking for a job. We were trying to find a way to feed our family, buy our toys, and pay the bills. Over the years we have often thought about whether or not we were doing what God intended us to do, but for many, it didn't matter—we were stuck. Wouldn't it have been easy if God had sent each of us an email or a text with his plans for our lives before we go so far into things? When you think about it, we are here for such a short time; knowing what God wanted us to do would save us a lot of time and energy.

We've been taught to think that dissatisfaction is a bad thing. It is such a terrible thing that we should do just about everything possible to avoid it. We should just ignore it? Maybe even act like it doesn't bother us at all. Many people have found another idea—just take a pill and plaster on a smile. Don't misunderstand; as we know dissatisfaction can often result from spiritual warfare and does not indicate that we are out of

God's will. It can, however, also signify that He has another purpose for you. So if you're miserable in your current career or job and you've prayed, sought counsel from others, and looked for guidance through scripture and you're still miserable; consider that God may have another plan. The world tells us to let our hearts be our guide. If it feels good, just do it! If you are having fun, making money, not hurting anyone, and caring for your family, you must have found why God put you here.

> *"Many are the plans in a person's heart, but it is the Lord's purpose that prevails."*
> *Proverbs 19:21*

We have all read about people who believe they must move globally to determine why they were put here. Who knows, they do. However, according to scripture, everyone's purpose in life is the same, but how we accomplish it is different. Our purpose is to glorify God; where and how have you been created to achieve this? While this often sounds easy, it has kept more people up at night than anything else. How were you made to glorify God? You may have been looking for that specific job you thought would define who you are and why you are here all this time, when in reality, you may be in the correct position now. Wherever you are planted, your focus must be to love God first and then love everyone else as we love ourselves; the question is how. Like many things in our lives, we often find that we are overcomplicating things. Some believe they need to change careers, marriage partners, find a different family, or change locations to find the reason for being here. Yet, in 1 Corinthians 10:31, the Apostle Paul said that we must *"do all to the glory of God no matter what we do."*

You may be exactly where Jesus needs you to be. But, unfortunately, the world wants you to believe that your job, children, or hobby is why you are here. When we are not satisfied with what we have, we look for something better. Do you know what the "open door" approach to finding God's will is? You wait until a door opens, assume God is opening it, and walk through it. The problem with this approach is God is not the only one who can open a door. Once we commit to studying the Word of God, we often become obsessed with trying to be obedient and ensure we are in his will. At some time, we have all prayed and asked God to give us clear directions to ensure we follow His will. We ponder if our pursuits are serving our purpose.

"And we know that in all things God works for the good of those who love him, who have been called according to his purpose."
Romans 8:28

What about you? What is your excuse for not discovering the reason you were created? What's your excuse for not developing your passion? The apostle Peter shares with us things that slow down this process: malice, deceit, hypocrisy, envy, and evil speaking. Peter says those things we must get rid of. Likewise, the writer of Hebrews says we need to "*lay aside every weight, and the sin which so easily ensnares us.*" The apostle Paul encourages us to avoid worldly wisdom. We are told, "*The wisdom of this world is foolishness with God.*" (1 Corinthians 3:19). Whatever is slowing down your growth and ability to identify and share your purpose in Christ should be put aside.

Notes From Reading:

____

____

____

____

Questions For The Group:

____

____

____

Prayer Request for Today:

____

____

____

Day 2

WHAT'S IMPORTANT TO YOU?

"A new commandment I give to you, that you love one another: just as I have loved you, you also are to love one another. By this, all people will know that you are my disciples if you have love for one another."
John 13:34-35

DAILY PRAYER

Lord Jesus, please help me reprioritize my life. You are essential, but I also love the things in my life. Please help me as I try to place you in the position you belong in. I know I am still supposed to care for and love my family, but help me reorder the way I think and act so that you are my top priority

.

What's really important to you? Let's assume no one will know your answer or see your notes from our study. Now, what are the top three most essential things in your life? We often talk about our priorities in life, but how often have you stopped to think about which of these crucial things are the most important? Take a moment and imagine that you're at the end of your life. You only have a few minutes to reflect on your life and decide what you should have done differently. What would tell yourself? Would it be something like, I should have spent more time doing..... Well guess what, we still have time to do what we have always wanted to do. Let's spend some time today reflecting on the essential things in our life. Our priorities often change throughout life, so reflecting on this often is necessary. Where would you place your relationship with Jesus on your list? Is He the top priority in your life, or is He somewhere behind your children, family, and friends? This week's scripture is intended to remind us that our relationship with Jesus is designed to be the essential relationship in our lives. This often seems impossible because so much emphasis is placed on our ranking in the parent of the year contest. Or making sure we will the employee of the year. Yet, scripture warns us not to put anything or anyone above our relationship with Jesus Christ.

Many believe their relationships with friends are the most important thing in their life. For others, work is at the top of their priority list. However, if married, your relationship with your spouse is called to be your second most important relationship. If either of these relationships ring a bell, it may mean that your priorities have slipped out of line. These relationships are undoubtedly vital to our happiness. Good friends, a committed spouse, and great children are relationships that we must thank God daily for. We tend to forge an inseparable bond with people we can always count on, no matter how dark things get. We desire people around us who can be our confidant, shoulder to lean on, and sometimes the voice of reason we need. We should always remember how fortunate we are to be surrounded by people we love.

"A new commandment I give to you that you love one another: just as I have loved you, you also are to love one another. By this, all people will know that you are my disciples if you have love for one another."
John 13:34-35

We know the importance of placing Jesus at the top of our priority list, but many things keep pushing Him back down. We hear about it if we don't spend time with our family or our job. However, if we don't spend the time we desire with Jesus, He simply waits His turn for when we find the time to fit Him in.

Your cell phone alarm goes off; you roll over, grab your phone, and see that you have several emails from work and more text than you can count. One of your friends tagged you on a post on Facebook, and before you know it, you are scarfing down breakfast and jumping in the shower in a mad dash for work. Driving to work, you promise that today, you will create more time to spend with Jesus. When you get to work, it is crazy. You have large projects pressing and everyone wants a minute of your time. Your friends are texting because today is your time to pick where the group will meet for lunch. Afternoon comes and goes, and you've decided you are too busy to even go to the gym. The kids have soccer and band practice and you need to go by the store to get something for dinner. And just like that, your day is done, and Jesus patiently continues to wait for his time with you. Tomorrow you'll get back on track and spend that time you promised Jesus. Does that sound at all familiar?

God has given you an internal guidance system. It's your responsibility to keep the main thing the main thing. People provide us with many opportunities to spend our time unproductively. We have to be cautious with their advice and motives. Jesus cautions us to be willing to give up whatever and whoever is keeping us from Him. One of the core beliefs is that Jesus should always come first in everything. Sometimes, that means we have to make some critical and often unpopular decisions. People try to convince us that something isn't that bad or that we can do something we know in our heart we shouldn't do. When that happens, we must put our relationship with Jesus above all else. We must be firm and clarify exactly where we stand, not allowing ourselves to be influenced by others.

When we feel forces to give up something we enjoy, we naturally want to hold on to it. So the next time you feel pressured to put things in front of your relationship with Jesus, stop and pray about what things or people are pulling you away from Him. Whoever or whatever they are probably don't even know they are a part of it—for example, your children. It's not your family's fault if you feel out of balance in your relationship with Jesus. You should be commended for the effort you put into your job with your spouse and family. Today, we are merely rethinking how to put Jesus back at the top of the list.

"And everyone who has left houses or brothers or sisters or father or mother or wife or children or lands, for My name's sake, shall receive a hundredfold and inherit eternal life."
Matthew 19:29

We hear it all the time— life is short. In a world of chaos, social media, and divisiveness, we have precious things that can quickly become overshadowed. Sometimes, circumstances are out of our control and they consume our time and attention. Sometimes, our choices cause us to misplace the things that mean the most. We have different needs and priorities, but we share one thing in common: the absence of Jesus at the center of our lives will cause us to feel incomplete. While our lives and priorities may differ, we must remember there is one thing vital to living a life of fulfillment… something we need to fight for… something that matters.

The disciples were standing on the shore of the Sea of Galilee. They had just finished a long night of fishing and had caught nothing. Jesus walks up, tells them to return, and casts their nets into deeper water. The Bible tells us that when they did, they caught so many fish that their nets were breaking. When they tried to placed all the fish in the boats, the boats began to sink. Jesus told them, *"From now on, I want you to be fishers of men."* We must realize what a life-changing decision this was for these early disciples. The Bible says, "Then they brought the boats to land, left everything, and followed him." They left everything and made Jesus the main thing. Think briefly about what they would have left behind that day. What are you willing to leave behind to make Jesus front and center in your life?

They left their jobs. It wasn't a hobby they did to relax; it was their livelihood. This was how they made a living and yet they quit their jobs immediately to follow Jesus. They even left their families because Mark speaks of Simon's mother-in-law, so we know Simon was married. So, this was not only a commitment for the disciples but for their families as well. They left their security, and all they knew to follow someone who had not even told them where they were going. One thing that happens when we decide to place Christ in His place is that we have to give up some of our control, which may not be easy for you. These men left their jobs, their families, and their sense of security; why? Because they chose to invest their lives in something much bigger. Instead of making their relationship with Jesus important, they made it the most important thing.

Jesus said "But seek first the Kingdom of God and His righteousness, and all these things will be added to you."
Matthew 6:33

The first step in prioritizing our life is to *"seek first the Kingdom of God."* Jesus wants us to know that His priorities must be our priorities. There is a show about people who trade in their large, expansive homes for "tiny houses." In this episode, a young lady downsized from her three-bedroom 2,200 square foot house and moved into a 384-square-foot tiny house. This move liberated her as she no longer had a mortgage, and her monthly bills were almost nothing. She purged many of her most prized possessions before moving. Old photos, love letters, and even her college letter jacket landed in the trash. What things do you need to purge that affect your relationship with Jesus? Let's commit today to striving to place Jesus at the top of our priorities. We can still love our spouse, adore our children, and have the most incredible friends in the world. But let's never forget who provided all those things to us.

Notes From Reading:

Questions For The Group:

Prayer Request for Today:

Day 3

MADE IN CHRIST'S IMAGE

"So God created man in his image, in the image of God he created him; male and female he created them."
Genesis 1:27

DAILY PRAYER

Dear God, help me prioritize my life so that I place studying your Word and desiring to live in your image at the top of my list. I want to study, but I need more time. So please help me find the time to learn your Word and discover what God wants me to be. Lord, I don't even know where to start.

God made you unique and that can sometime be frightening. The Bible specifically tells us that God created us in His image, but what does that mean? How do you feel about yourself today? You should feel great. You were made in the image of Jesus Christ. Yet, for some reason, low self-esteem is a problem that is sweeping our country. How can we feel bad about ourselves when we were created in the image of Almighty God? According to The Self Esteem Book by Dr. Joe Rubino, 85% of the world's population is affected by low self-esteem. We all need to listen very carefully to the truth. You are someone extraordinary. God made you, and He made you in His image. One of the main reasons people struggle with having healthy self-worth is they don't fully grasp what it means to be made in God's image. Like Adam and Eve, we will always struggle with sin and failure; however, we must remember that God considers us unique. Interestingly, many people today face great battles concerning how they view themselves. Ninety percent of all people surveyed in a recent poll would like to change at least one aspect of their physical appearance. How about you?

It is still disappointing how many people believe that man and woman just appeared on Earth through some cosmic explosion and that God had nothing to do with it. Our children study evolution and the Big Bang theory in school, and some believe these things are the real reasons we all came into existence. Scripture says we are created in the image of Christ, but does that mean we look like Him? Does it mean He made us have a heart like His? We often need help with the idea of what it means to be made in the image of Jesus. God is of tremendous and immeasurable worth, so human beings made in his image must also be of great value. The most obscure person is not ordinary in God's eyes. Being made in the image of God provides the basis for our life. If we are made in the image of God, we share His characteristics.

"Let us make man in our image, according to our likeness; let them have dominion over the fish of the sea, over the birds of the air, and over the cattle, over all the Earth and over every creeping thing that creeps on the Earth. So God created man in His image; in the image of God, He created him; male and female He created them."
Genesis 1:26-27

Few questions are more significant than what it means to be an image-bearer of God. It's at the heart of what it means to be a Christian. It governs our ethics, calling us to see every person (not just those like us or those we like) as valuable and treat everyone with dignity, respect, and honor. It helps us answer questions like:

- What makes human life valuable?
- Where does our worth, dignity, and value come from?

- How should we talk to, treat, interact, and relate to other people?

The Biblical testimony is that God made men and women with a uniqueness that is not present in the other things He created. Only men and women were created in God's image and had this extraordinary honor and privilege. Only humanity had God breathe life into them. We are unique among all creations. Scientists tell us there are a hundred thousand million stars in the Milky Way and millions upon millions of galaxies. If we ponder these types of facts, we can easily find ourselves feeling very insignificant. The universe we live in is beyond our comprehension, and the God who made the stars and everything else made you. Yet, amid this overwhelming universe, God made you in a way that sets you apart from everything He created. You are not a product of chance. God specifically created you, and He knew you before you were born! He knows your name!

"I am fearfully and wonderfully made."
Psalm 139

Knowing that God created each person uniquely and knew you before birth, how should we deal with issues such as abortions, disposal, and physician-assisted suicide? Do we have a right to act against what is created in God's image? When God created man in His image, He said we would resemble God in ways other than a physical likeness. He designed us not like animals but capable of facial expressions corresponding to emotional feelings, and a brain and tongue capable of articulating symbolic speech. In addition, God gave us intellectual ability that is far superior to that of any animal. We are given a mind capable of hearing and understanding God's communication with us, emotions capable of responding to God in love and devotion, and a will that enables us to choose whether or not to obey God.

When a former Chicago mayor was concerned about violence in the city's housing projects, she did a surprising thing—she moved into one of them. She lived for twenty days in an apartment in the dangerous community of Cabrini Green. While her action sparked controversy, her decision to live among Chicago's poorest citizens also drew needed attention to a long-neglected neighborhood. The Gospel of John focuses on how God came to dwell among us. John takes us to the beginning— not just when Jesus was born on Earth but back to the beginning of time. The Son of God did not begin to exist at His physical birth; He was present at the creation: *"In the beginning was the Word, and the Word was with God, and the Word was God."* (John 1:10). John stakes a claim: Jesus is God. Jesus coexisted with His Father from the beginning.

"The Word became flesh and made his dwelling among us. We have seen his glory, the glory of the one and only Son, who came from the Father, full of grace and truth."
John 1:14

As much as we often desire to break the world into little groups, denominations, cultures, races, etc., the truth is that we are all one species bound together on Earth, and we are more alike than different. Therefore, dividing ourselves into groups is a sad and self-serving endeavor in the vast scheme of life. God's love is for everyone because regardless of where we come from, we were all created in His image, irrespective of who we are. We don't want to be phony Christians who turn the world off because we only want to be with people like us. Non-believers can smell a fake. Years ago, a new missionary went to Venezuela for the first time. He struggled with the language and didn't understand most of what happened. He visited a local church and took the only spot available—on the front row—because he arrived late. Trying not to make a fool of himself, he followed the man's actions sitting next to him. The man clapped his hands as they sang, and the missionary clapped. When the man stood to pray, the missionary stood also. When the man sat, he sat as well. During the preaching, the missionary didn't understand a word. He sat and tried to look just like the man next to him. Then he perceived the preacher was giving announcements. People clapped, so he looked to see if the man was clapping. He was, and so he applauded as well. Smiling, the preacher said something else. When the man stood, the missionary jumped to his feet. A hush fell over the congregation. A few people gasped. He looked around, and no one was standing. After the service, the preacher stood at the door, shaking the hands of those leaving. When the missionary greeted the preacher, the preacher said, in English: I take it you don't speak Spanish. The missionary said, No, I don't. Is it that obvious? Well, yes, said the preacher. I announced that the Rodriguez family had a newborn baby boy and would the proud father please stand up- and you did!

How beautiful is it to think that God, the Creator of the universe, made us? He looked at us and called us His masterpiece. We shouldn't just observe the inherent value but work to view it in those around us. We should walk confidently, knowing that our Creator makes no mistakes and loves and sees us as beautiful.

"For we are God's handiwork, created in Christ Jesus to do good works, which God prepared us to do."
Ephesians 2:10

This verse doesn't just talk about us being God's handiwork but declares we each are called to fulfill good works. We are so valuable that God entrusted tasks for each of us to accomplish His kingdom's betterment. God has gifted us with unique talents and abilities; therefore, your calling will look different from someone else's. There is no need for comparison between us and others. We should only continually strive to reflect Jesus Christ by living by His Word and pursuing our specific calling. If we are made in His image, shouldn't the way we live reflect Him?

Notes From Reading:

Questions For The Group:

Prayer Request for Today:

Day 4

A NEW CREATION

"...and put on the new self, which in the likeness of God has been created in righteousness and holiness of the truth."
Ephesians 4:24

DAILY PRAYER

Jesus, please help me to be the person you created me to be. I want those around me to see the difference you are making in my life. Change me from the person I have been. Reorder my priorities in life. Jesus, I need help because the only person I know how to be is the one I have been. I want to be a new creation in you. Please help me follow your example and resist the pull of this broken world.

We all strongly desire to be ourselves and live our own life. Unfortunately, we live in a world where people often worry simply about themselves and disregard how they may clash with others. Should the world see a significant difference in your life because you love Jesus? When we become Christian, we are called to be a different creation, and our lives must show this decisive and sometimes drastic change. We all desire to start over sometimes. Giving our life to Christ is just this chance to start fresh. If you want to see a remarkable change in your life, today is the day for you to become that new creation. Our lives are changing, however, it is often happening so subtly that most of us don't even notice. We are all getting pulled into collecting as many toys we can accumulate as we travel through life. What matters most to God isn't what we do or what we have; it's who we are. So, pursuing specific accomplishments in life isn't nearly as important as becoming the new, better person God desires. Instead, we must use our time and energy wisely but focus on living up to our potential and growing into the person God wants us to be. Becoming a new person means letting go of what has filled your life and filling it with love and joy. So, how do you become the person God wants you to be?

"Therefore, if anyone is in Christ, he is a new creation; old things have passed away; behold, all things have become new. Now all things are of God, who has reconciled us to Himself through Jesus Christ and has given us the ministry of reconciliation, that is, that God was in Christ reconciling the world to Himself, not imputing their trespasses to them, and has committed to us the word of reconciliation."
2 Corinthians 5:17-19

We learn that a person is a new creation when we are in Christ. "*But God forbid that I should boast except in the cross of our Lord Jesus Christ, by whom the world has been crucified to me and the world. In Christ Jesus, neither circumcision nor uncircumcision avails anything but a new creation.*" (Galatians 6:14-15) So, how do you become a new creation? "*For you are all sons of God through faith in Christ Jesus. For as many of you as were baptized into Christ have put on Christ.*" (Galatians 3:26-27) When we act through faith and are baptized, we enter into Christ. Paul also connects the new creation or new life to baptism in his letter to the Romans. "*Therefore we were buried with Him through baptism into death, that just as Christ was raised from the dead by the glory of the Father, even so, we also should walk in newness of life.*" (Romans 6:4) Therefore, this change comes about when you accept Christ.How have you changed? The significant change is that "old things have passed away."

"If indeed you have heard Him and have been taught by Him, as the truth is in Jesus: that you put off, concerning your former conduct, the old man which grows corrupt according to the deceitful lusts, and be renewed in the spirit of your mind, and that you put on the new man which was created according to God, in true righteousness and holiness."
Ephesians 4:21-24

Therefore, it is a conscious behavior change because our sins are removed. "*But now you yourselves are to put off all these: anger, wrath, malice, blasphemy, filthy language out of your mouth. Do not lie to one another, since you have put off the old man with his deeds and have put on the new man who is renewed in knowledge according to the image of Him who created him, where there is neither Greek nor Jew, circumcised nor uncircumcised, barbarian, Scythian, enslaved person nor free, but Christ is all and in all.*" (Colossians 3:8-11) God has already created a new self for you. You are not a different person; you are a new creation and your best self. You are all that God made you to be. Your character, personality, capabilities, and passions are changed in what Paul calls your "new self." Paul uses the imagery of new clothing. (Ephesians 4:22-24) It is like a new outfit hanging in our closet. You could put it on; although it is not the kind you have worn before, it might even be scary to wear it in public because you are not sure how people will react. Yet we know it is much better than what we usually wear, so we put it on! Of course, the new self God has for us goes much deeper than what is on the outside; it goes to the core of who we are. If Paul were writing today, he might be talking about a software upgrade or even a significant update of your operating system.

Our new self comes with unique passions and a new attitude toward life. Our perspective becomes like Jesus: we have a great love for people, a servant's heart, strength in facing evil, and a desire to please the Father. Think about what a difference this can make as you face the challenges and opportunities of life. In addition, the new self accepts the righteousness of Christ as God's gracious gift, freeing you to be honest about who you are and what you do. When did your children or grandchildren last catch you talking with Jesus? Today is the day to start allowing yourself to act the way Christ intended for you to act. Take off your baggage and ask God to help you be the new creation He promised.

"But one thing I do: Forgetting what is behind and straining toward what is ahead, I press on toward the goal to win the prize for which God has called me heavenward in Christ Jesus."
Philippians 3:13-14

Jesus is not interested in all your past mistakes but in the new person you are becoming. The Apostle Paul teaches us a great lesson about looking ahead rather than dwelling on the past. But that doesn't mean Paul developed amnesia while in the Roman jail. Instead, he remembered his history and recognized the man he once was. However, he didn't let his past discourage or defeat him. He was determined to press on and to keep running the race. Paul was focused on eternity and what awaited him at the end of his life. We've all made mistakes and have a past that we can't change. Maybe the error was an affair, something you said, or an addiction. We commonly view our lives as past, present, future. The Bible suggests that we consider time flowing from the future into the present and then into the past. As a new creation, we should be future-oriented, forgetting what lies behind us. Have you ever noticed how mired down in the here and now we often become? Sometimes, it's dark and scary, and we're fumbling around because we feel like we have lost control because of broken relationships, money problems, and illnesses. Paul was focused on the future. He pressed toward the upward call of God in Christ Jesus. Paul used the image of a race to describe the Christian life. In (Philippians 3:12), Paul wrote, "*I press on.*" In verse 14, he wrote, "*I press toward the goal.*" The word press means to run swiftly to catch a person or thing, to run after. Paul was focused on the future and the person he could become.

You may be one of the millions that enjoy social media. Often people like to keep up with family and friends while seeing the new creative ideas other people come up with. However, a recent article revealed spending extended time on social media makes people worried, lonely, and unhappy. Being on the site also increases feelings of discontent as users compare their lives to others. One researcher wrote, We want to learn about other people and have others learn about us—but through that very learning process, we may start to resent what others have. Perhaps a negative part of the human condition is the urge to compare ourselves to others to find how we measure up. It's hard to move forward in our new life if we can't let go of our old one. Discontent, loneliness, and jealousy usually stem from our focus on ourselves. We find absolute joy when we are allowed to change and shed our old lives. Today, ask God to turn our hearts and minds away from yourself and help you to become a new creation—away from who you are and more into who He wants you to become.

"They came to John and said to him, Rabbi, that man who was with you on the other side of the Jordan—the one you testified about—look, he is baptizing, and everyone is going to him. To this, John replied, A person can receive only what is given to them from Heaven. You yourselves can testify that I said, I am not the Messiah but am sent ahead of him."
John 3:26-28

John the Baptist's disciples, expressed similar discontent and jealousy. People became upset because others went to Jesus to be baptized instead of going to John. They viewed it as a competition. John was quick to set them straight. He clarified his position concerning Jesus by saying, "*I am not the Messiah but am sent ahead of him.*" He asserted that his decreasing popularity was exactly as it was meant: "*He must become greater; I must become less.*" John compared himself to an attendant at a wedding. He was never meant to be the main attraction. How wonderful it is that God is in the improvement business. We have all wandered away from God; the world has left us broken, dirty, and need serious help.

A wonderful Christian couple—Chip and JoAnn Gaines—have a television show called Fixer Upper. Their show's tagline is: We take the worst house in the best neighborhood and turn it into our client's dream home. I love to watch this show because of the interaction between Chip and JoAnn with their children and also because they are not ashamed of their faith. As incredible as the Gaines' ability and giftedness are, as impressive as it is to see what they can do with old homes needing restoration, God does so much more with us when He restores us to our new creation. He can take that which is ugly and make it beautiful in His image. He can assume the worst of sinners and transform us into the best of saints. God never does a patch job, fixing and repairing just parts of who we are—He always does a complete restoration, inside and out. His work is terrific, and when He is finished, we are not the same person we were when He started. God takes what is useless and falling apart and makes it solid and loyal in Him to do things of eternal significance. And unlike the homes restored on Fixer Upper, which will one day begin to deteriorate and wear out, we have been given an eternal fixing up by God.

So how does this work? It's one thing to believe in Jesus but another to make Him Lord of your life. Invite Jesus into your heart and ask Him to cleanse you of your sins. If you believe that Jesus died on the cross for your sins and that He is the Son of God (the awaited Messiah), then you will be saved. We must spend time in God's presence and His Word because faith comes by hearing the Word (Romans 10:17). Real transformation and decisions/choices/lifestyle changes are made when our thinking is appropriately aligned. Prayer is vital, as well. Let's not just give God an extensive request list, but in the stillness of our devotion time, we must listen to God in our spirit. This will happen if we carve out the time and seek Him genuinely. We must confess your sins and turn from your old ways and we know this doesn't happen overnight. You may have s testimony of being delivered from drug abuse, alcohol addiction, and many other things. Sometimes, this will take time, but God is faithful. If we choose to obey, He will bless our lives. Those who honor God will be honored. When we resist the devil, He shall flee.

It is important to stay around like-minded believers. How can we flourish in the things of God if we are walking with people who don't desire to serve God? If we want to be a professional dancer, we hang with dancers at dance studios; you take classes and work hard. If we're going to be a singer, we practice, do exercises, rehearse, etc. If we want to be a firm believer and change, we need to learn from the Bible, apply it, and be around others doing the same thing. We must stay in worship and guard your mind, ears, and hearts. What we think about, we do, and what we do, we become. Don't you want to be known as a solid follower of Jesus? Don't you want to leave a legacy of being a disciple of Jesus? Don't you want to fall at His feet in worship and thank Him for all that He has done? Seriously, we are so blessed. We have our health, salvation, friends, family, schools, jobs, a roof over our heads, cars, computers, and phones…we have more than enough.

Notes From Reading:

____

____

____

____

Questions For The Group:

____

____

____

Prayer Request for Today:

____

____

____

Day 5

SERVING OTHERS

"God is not unjust; he will not forget your work and the love you have shown him as you have helped his people and continue to help them."
Hebrews 6:10

DAILY PRAYER

God, help me to find my calling to serve others. This is important, but I need more time to do it regularly. I want to be your servant, but I need clarification on what that means. Please place me in the situations you wish me to serve the people you want me to help. I love you so much; I don't know when or how to serve you.

The new national theme song should be What's In This For Me? It seems that fewer and fewer are thinking about servanthood except at Christmas or when a federal disaster takes the front stage. People always step up to volunteer to help others but it often takes a major tragedy to get our attention. Still, our society seems to imply, It is better to take care of yourself than worry about those who don't take care of themselves. Nothing is more central to Christians than our desire and need to serve others. Jesus came to Earth to be a servant, and we are called to be servants as well. Being called by God is often thought to be something only missionaries, pastors, nuns, and a few church leaders experience. The Bible, however, says everyone is "called to serve God" —by serving others. We are not saved by serving, but we are called to serving. It is interesting how many people embrace their belief that helping others is their ticket to eternal life. While their service is noble and commendable, a real disappointment is waiting.

"For even the Son of Man did not come to be served, but to serve, and to give his life as a ransom for many."
Mark 10:45

Jesus didn't come wanting others to serve Him; instead, He served everyone. A Chinese saying proclaims, If you want happiness for an hour, take a nap. If you want happiness for a day, go fishing. If you want happiness for a year, inherit a fortune. If you want happiness for a lifetime, help somebody. For centuries, some of the greatest thinkers have suggested that happiness is found in helping others. Today, the mass media is trying to convince us that people are only motivated by self-interest. We are taught that acting rationally is to maximize what we desire for ourselves. Values such as—service, duty, allegiance to others, morality, and shared ideals—are often presented as irrelevant or at least negligible. Studies continue to indicate we receive a stronger sense of purpose and meaning when serving others. A local newspaper recently headlined a young woman who spends her spring breaks in the African bush treating AIDS patients. When we read articles such as this, we often think about what we can offer in comparison. Most certainly can't take off for an extended period and go to Africa. Even if we did, would we know what to do? The answer is more straightforward than we think: a lot.

We can't be intimidated and feel we are competing against others when serving people. Small choices—little steps—often lead to significant change. If you asked the girl volunteering in Africa, she'd probably be able to trace back a trail of small choices and decisions that led her there, one step at a time. She probably didn't just suddenly go from never having served to boarding a plane for Africa. We are called for different purposes—some more dramatic than others, but not necessarily more important. The mission field is not limited to far-off places—it includes our home, city, work, and home. Wherever we are, God has something vital going on. There are two kinds of people in our world: those that help others and those that don't. God said that His followers should be helpers and we are commanded to serve others. God created us so that we will not find fulfillment until we are helping others. Unfortunately, even though God designed us to serve, we have difficulty making time available. Jesus took the time to teach the disciples about servanthood; however, today, we know it is essential; we can't seem to find the time.

What do you believe was the motive for the Disciples to follow Jesus? Was it honor, glory, or power? Looking at their early lives, these things seemed on their minds. When the Disciples began following Jesus, their motivation seemed to experience God more deeply and meaningfully. As they realized that Jesus was about restoring the Kingdom of God on Earth, their motives drifted to things like power, honor, and glory. When we think about being a servant, we must also be aware of this. Within us, we all have a deep desire to be honored, experience glory, be essential, and be served. It's so natural we see people vying for position and prestige almost everywhere we look. If we embrace the power of helping others, we must check our motives before we begin. Even if we desire to serve others, we can't find the time to do it. God placed us in time, at this exact time, and will take us home when He chooses. The Lord put us here to make an eternal difference, and serving others is essential to Him. What are you being called to do?

"As long as it is the day, we must do the works of him who sent me. The night is coming when no one can work."
John 9:4

In 1974, Harry Chapin released a song titled The Cats in the Cradle. The song told the story of a dad who could never find the time to do things with his son as he was growing up. Later, when his child became an adult, he couldn't find time for his dad. So, how will we make time to serve others?

Robert Moffett, a great missionary, once said, We shall have all eternity in which to celebrate our victories, but only one short hour before the sun sets in which to win them. We have only a few days to make a difference in this world. We must stay on track, follow God's lead, and stay focused.

Don't you love the story of Jesus at the wedding in Cana? His mother mentions the wine problem to Jesus. He hasn't performed any miracles up to this point, so she's probably not expecting Him to start then. However, Jesus did have a reputation for fixing difficult situations. As his mother, she had a lot of faith in Him. Jesus doesn't show much response to His mother's hint. "What does this have to do with Me? My hour has not yet come." I'm sure Mary knew her Son well, and instead of arguing or giving up, she turned to the servants and said, "Do whatever He tells you." And off she went, leaving the problem in Jesus' hands. As Mary anticipated, Jesus got to work on the situation— although maybe not exactly how she had imagined. He performed His first miracle. He didn't do it alone by magically causing the wineskins to refill themselves. No, Jesus had a better idea. He made service a part of His miracle. *"Fill the jars with water,"* He said. Jesus asked them to do it, which was good enough for them and should also be good enough for us.

Learning what God wants us to do and how He wants us to serve requires that we spend time with Him in His Word. Jesus knows all the things we are dealing with. He, too, was tempted, betrayed, hungry, tired, misunderstood, and falsely accused. Christ has promised to be in our midst and never leave us. He also promises to be with us when we serve in uncomfortable areas. We can count on one thing for sure: He is already there. Serving with Christ doesn't mean just handing out meals or giving money. There is a never-ending need to serve our fellow man.

"Mourn with those who mourn."
Romans 12:15

Our communities are full of people that are sick and hurting. How great it will be one day to have no more needy people, no beggars, and no worried widows. Wouldn't that be a great way to live today? Unfortunately, selfishness has a way of infecting us all. It accounts for much of what we say and do. The cure to greed is to have the serving mind of Christ. By God's grace, we should not stand far off in fear or disgust from anyone. Instead, we must pray to God, trusting His promise that they shall all be comforted. Sometimes, the idea of serving intimidates us. We must avoid falling into the trap that we have nothing to offer. We all have things to offer. Just in case you need a few ideas to get you started, take a look at some ways you can serve:

Be kind to strangers. The best way to serve God and others is to be kind. Smile. Don't snap at the sales clerk for taking too long. Don't demand to have your way. Don't berate the telemarketer. Don't be a road rage-filled driver.

Remember someone. Send a birthday card or gift to a lonely widow or widower. Let them know their special day is still unique. Call someone who feels under the weather, is going through a difficult time, or is experiencing a grievous loss.

Pray for those in need. Don't generalize your prayers. Be specific. Pray for _____, who is experiencing the rigors of boot camp. Pray for _____, who is experiencing a difficult pregnancy. Pray for _____ and _____, who are trying to be patient while waiting for the call to travel to South Korea to finalize their little girl's adoption. Pray for the leaders of our nation by name.

Share food. Invite a college student to your home for dinner. Fix snacks for the high school youth group to enjoy during their Bible study. Fix a meal for a new mom, the people who just moved into the neighborhood, or someone just home from the hospital. Bake cookies, bread, or pies to give to first-time visitors at your church.

Share your time. Sit and read to an older adult. Take someone to and from their doctor's appointment or chemo treatment—volunteer to help the church secretary with some of her duties at church. Offer to prepare class materials for Sunday school teachers. Read to the children at a daycare.

Share your stuff. Donate sports equipment, clothing, and household items to shelters, children's homes, and other organizations. Host a Bible study in your home (even if you aren't the one teaching it). Invite the youth group to enjoy the pool in your backyard or the horses on your farm. Give away part of your garden's produce.

Share your talents. Teach a Bible study. Offer to do hair and nails for the high school girls at church for prom. Babysit for young parents so they can enjoy a date night now and then. Perform car maintenance and handyman chores for the elderly in the church and your neighborhood. Tutor a child or children struggling in school. Help a young couple set up a reasonable budget. Teach others how to garden, sew, or whatever you are good at.

Share the Word. Leave a devotional or a Bible on the table at a restaurant. Ask people how you can pray for them and help them… then do it.

"Let us not become weary in doing good, for at the proper time, we will reap a harvest if we do not give up."
Galatians 6:9

Notes From Reading:

Questions For The Group:

Prayer Request for Today:

Day 6

YOU ARE UNIQUE

"For as in one body we have many members, and the members do not all have the same function, so we, though many, are one body in Christ, and individually members one of another."

Romans 12:4-5

DAILY PRAYER

Jesus, please help me see the uniqueness of those around me. Please help me identify and appreciate the differences between my family and friends. I must be reminded that every person I encounter, even those I am not particularly close to, is created in Jesus Christ's image. How can I treat people as I sometimes do when we are all made in His image?

There are some strange people in this world. Have you ever thought about how different people are? It seems crazy that we were all created to be unique, yet we spend so much of our lives trying to be like someone else. Do you try to dress like someone else, have a similar car, or own a house equal to your friends? Society separates and labels people that stand out as being different. People wearing different clothes or hairstyles are often singled out as strange. Wear your hair with a color different from the masses and listen to people talk. While we live in a time that says we are individuals, and it is OK to be different, we often spend a lot of time trying to fit in and be just like everybody else. Have you ever wondered how parents have multiple children, yet each one is so incredibly different? Each child has the same mother and Father, grows up in the same environment, and yet acts like they could be part of another family. We are all very different and we were created that way purposefully. This is one of the miracles of life—no two people are the same. We all have something that makes us stand out. Yet, we all share one major thing in common: we are made in the image of Jesus. Shouldn't that mean that although we are unique, we are more alike than we think?

"I praise you, for I am fearfully and wonderfully made. Wonderful are your works; my soul knows it very well."
Psalms 139:14

People are different, and our passion for things is different. A prize possession to one person is junk to another. Someone's comfortable temperature is someone else's sweltering heat. One person's bright illumination is someone else's blinding light. We act differently because we perceive, think, feel, want, need, react, and judge differently. Unfortunately, the older we get, the more we underestimate how different we are. This implies a few things; it means that we don't always understand others as much as we think we do—why they do what they do and the intent of their actions and words. And other people don't understand us as well as we think they should. Every person is a unique puzzle composed of pieces of personality, life experiences, knowledge, and emotions. Each of us has our perspective and values, primarily fueled by how we have been raised, experienced, and navigated the world. Regardless of our life's path, the journey leaves its mark. We all have something unique and valuable to contribute to the world. We might enjoy the same food, share hobbies, or hold similar beliefs or opinions as other people. What makes us different from all others is not these things alone but the combination of all these things that only we have. We are unique.

We share many things in common with others; however, we are essentially one of a kind. No one has been given the same makeup as God gave you. Your face, fingerprints, voice, and genetic makeup are matched by no one else's. Likewise, God has handcrafted you with your personality, talents, and motivations. That means one thing — you have an individual purpose in life that no one else can fulfill. We don't have to travel far to discover God's love for diversity and variety. Think about it: God made over 300,000 species of just spiders. Did you know that in one cubic foot of snow, there are 18 million individual snowflakes, not one of them alike? And while we can't tell the difference, it's snow to us; God created each of them. God likes variety in people, too. If you have ever waited in an airport or stood in line at Walmart, you have seen all sorts of unique and different people, none of them alike. God made every one of us individually, and when we look in the mirror, we see just how different we are. There's no one else like you in the entire world. You are one and only, and God broke the mold after he made you. He doesn't create carbon copies, only originals. You are unique to God. You matter to Him.

"Before I formed you in the womb, I knew you; before you were born, I consecrated you; I appointed you a prophet to the nations."
Jeremiah 1:5

Due to this uniqueness, you were created for a specific purpose. God created everything in the world for a purpose. You're not merely the result of a biological process. God made you for a reason. He designed you. God didn't just sit down and randomly access many components and put them together; then you came out. God purposefully and personally designed you.

Do you enjoy going to the beach? Have you ever seen photographs of individual grains of sand blown up by a microscope? Some grains look like red, polished stones, while others look like icicles. Some resemble speckled yellow and brown eggs; others are shaped like corncobs, snowflakes, and precious gems. Some grains are square, some spherical, and some are flat. No two grains are the same. And you'd never know you were even looking at grains of sand if no one told you. So the next time you sink your toes into the warm sand, think about every tiny grain, unique in shape, depth, color, and texture. God created every one of this infinite variety of grains. Because God shows off His creative abilities in tiny bits of sand, think about how much more He has done—and can do—with you, the crown of His creation. Too often, however, we try to model ourselves after another person. Whether the object of our admiration is a friend, celebrity, or stranger—we lose ourselves trying to be like someone else. The Lord knows why each grain of sand is a certain way, and He knows the same about you. Therefore, you must seek God through His Word to help you determine why you have your characteristics and what purpose He has in mind.

"For we are his workmanship, created in Christ Jesus for good works, which God prepared beforehand, that we should walk in them."
Ephesians 2:10

The feeling of inadequacy affects all of us to some degree and is a common human trait. Another trait is to fake it till you make it; both show we are not insufficient. Have you ever started a new job and acted like you knew more than you did? Have you been in a class only to discover it is far beyond your abilities? Hence, you try to appear at the same level as everyone else? Have you ever had to give a speech or present a program before a group and be uncomfortable at the thought of doing such a thing? If you were in any of these groups, you would fit in nicely with every other person on Earth. Although inadequacy is a common condition, it is the causal factor for countless adverse effects in our lives. Inadequacy can lead to compensating by lying, deceiving, addictions, overworking, and materialism. Inadequacy can be and is, for many, a devastating condition. We don't have the same talents as everyone else because God didn't give us those talents. He gave us unique skills.

Everyone has their quirks; some are good, and some are frustrating. If you embrace yourself for the good and the bad, you can become even more likable. Don't go with the crowd! It's the path less traveled by where all the hidden treasures lie. Maybe life is uncertain for you now, but you can regain control of your life by being who God made you be. The tremendous evangelical preacher Billy Graham was once asked a question. This question and his response are worth considering.

Q: I wish God had made me a different person. I'm ordinary, without talents or special abilities, and my life isn't fascinating. Other people get all the breaks. Why is life so unfair? — D.F.

A: Let me ask you a question: Did God make a mistake when he made you the way you are? Did he forget what he was doing and leave something out when he made you? No, of course not. God knew what he was doing and made you exactly how he wanted you to be. Furthermore, you are unique; no one else is exactly like you. (Think how dull the world would be if we were all exactly alike!) Even before you were born, God knew all about you, and he had a specific plan for you. God's words to Jeremiah apply to every one of us:

*"Before I formed you in the womb I knew you, before you
were born I set you apart."*
Jeremiah 1:5

You may not be a pro athlete or celebrity on the Forbes 100 richest family list. Still, God gave you specific gifts and abilities, and the most fulfilling thing you can do is discover them and use them for His glory. Begin by believing the most important truths you will ever know: God loves you, and Christ gave his life to you. By faith, open your heart and life to Him today and ask God to help you become the person He created you to be. Don't let envy or jealousy or anything else keep you from His plan for your life. Instead, keep your eyes on Christ. The Bible says, *"Be content with what you have, because God has said, Never will I leave you."* (Hebrews 13:5)

"But even the hairs of your head are all numbered."
Matthew 10:30

Christ calls us to be different! And it isn't about us; it's about Him. Christ teaches us a set of values and ideals distinctive from the world. He calls us to be different, to be counter-cultural. We are not to get our cue from those around us but from Him, and we are to prove to be genuine children of our heavenly Father. Advertisers seize any opportunity to appeal to the me obsessed generation. After all, who are you more likely to trust? The pretty face of an anonymous model or the picture of someone you know and love? It has become routine for celebrities to broadcast trivial information and fill Twitter with the insignificant moments that constitute their day, the implicit principle being that nothing is mundane once you are important enough. This delusion then spills out to the non-celebrity; recording ordinary events becomes proof of your importance.

Our Lord is gracious and compassionate and has rescued us through Jesus Christ, our Lord! He helps us in our struggles. He will allow us to avoid the hindrance of pride and fear of being different from the world around us! He helps us to be salt, light, and hope in a broken world. We must encourage one another to give Him our all in humility and a teachable spirit daily. Let's encourage each other to dig deep into the Word of God, which will equip us through the Holy Spirit. Let's run together, the race God has marked out for us, fixing our eyes on Jesus, the author and perfecter of our faith! Let's embrace being different!

Notes From Reading:

Questions For The Group:

Prayer Request for Today:

DAY 7

A LIFE OF FAITH

"I have been crucified with Christ, and I no longer live, but Christ lives in me. The life I now live in the body, I live by faith in the Son of God, who loved and gave himself for me."
Galatians 2:20

DAILY PRAYER

"Jesus, it is often hard to believe we were crucified in the garden with you on that late afternoon. That you died so we can live is so amazing that I often can't understand. I know you live in me through the Holy Spirit, but I often ignore Him. I try to solve my problems but forget you are always with me. Please help me to lean on you and stop trying to do things myself."

We are born with the desire to control situations and often like to do things our way and on our schedule. Unfortunately, one of the significant problems of our time is that Christians have been passive and have failed to stand up for what is important to Jesus in our world. Once we accept Jesus into our hearts and lives, He makes us a promise. He promises never to leave us and that the Holy Spirit will live in us forever. Have you ever wanted to go to a place you knew you shouldn't go to, to do something you know you shouldn't do? How about having an inappropriate discussion or encounter with someone you know you shouldn't be meeting with? Because of your relationship with Jesus, He lives within you, everywhere you go. Your life is His life, and we serve Him through our faith. We can't take a break from Him while we do what we may want to do. He is always with us.

A few years ago, a national home improvement store produced a commercial showing a proud do-it-yourself-er rewiring an old ceiling light in his living room. After he finished, he proudly gave the light one last turn, climbed off the aluminum ladder, and stepped aside to turn on the switch. When he turns it on, he stands with his hands on his hips and chest out, proudly satisfied with his brilliant work. Within a second of the light coming on, the outlet sparks, and the entire fixture falls to the floor, crushing a priceless antique table on its way down. The scene cuts away to the outside of the house, looking through the clear bay window of the room where the man is standing. Suddenly, the light fixture flies through the picture window and lands in the yard. The words flash on the screen: "Need help?" Doing it yourself in home improvement only sometimes works, which is also true in your personal life. We are all in desperate need of help when it comes to overcoming sinful habits and attitudes that keep us in bondage. To attempt to continue doing it yourself only leads to further frustration and disaster. Our faith is not a religion; it is a way of life. We must desire nothing to do with things that would cause us to stray from Biblical authority. To the Christian, this means the absolute death of our ego and a complete revival of our desire to live for Christ.

Satan hates it when we express our faith in prayer, go to church, or attend Bible study. While he hates these things, what he hates the most is when we pray. If we stop this one thing, Satan would be happy. We are not people who are given a one-time assignment and then sent out independently to do our best. As followers of Christ, we must stay connected every day, all day long. Paul said we are to "Pray without ceasing." That's how we experience His power, presence, and person.

At a dinner to honor Jesus, Mary anointed Him with expensive perfume made from the essence of nard. Mary's perfume cost the equivalent of a whole year's salary for a laborer in ancient Israel. Some Bible teachers believe the perfume Mary used to anoint Jesus was her perfume—a treasure, her most precious possession, she had been keeping for her wedding. Mary's generous gift to Jesus invoked strong negative responses. Some dinner guests rebuked her harshly, but Jesus commended her. Mary had done a "beautiful" thing. She had placed the perfume on Jesus to prepare Him for His death. (Mark 14:8) Leading up to this time, He had often said that He would be betrayed, killed, buried, and He would rise again. His disciples didn't seem to believe Him, for they didn't want it to happen. But Mary had been listening to Jesus and acting according to what she heard. Believing His words, she lovingly ministered to Him in His last week before He went to the cross. She gave her very best to honor Him.

Have you struggled with doubts about your faith? Do you deal with unanswered questions? Despite all the unanswered questions, we have chosen to live by faith, not sight. In doing so, we've genuinely witnessed how patient, just, loving, and amazing our God is. Some of us have been Christian for a long time, but we may struggle to find God in your everyday life. Some maybe silently questioning what we believe. So, how can we "live by faith" in a world that tells us "seeing is believing?" Our society has become accustomed to needing proof of something to believe it is true. Others tend to dismiss it if we can't explain it logically within our scope of human understanding. To dismiss faith on the premise of logic is to ignore the point of faith. Faith defies our worldly logic and earthly sense. God succeeds where our worldly logic fails! When we believe and have faith in what we do not see, God will reveal Himself to us in ways that are undeniably, inexplicably, and unimaginably the work of something bigger and more significant than ourselves. He does this through His creation, our innate moral compass and human conscience, His Word, His Son Jesus, and, among believers, through the leading and direction of the Holy Spirit. We can read famous authors who have presented their case for Christ and for having faith in what we do not see. The truth is, we will never have all the answers. The Bible explains that there will never be conclusive evidence to prove that He is the Creator to all humankind. He has ordained that some questions remain unanswered, forcing us to lean on our faith. We will always have questions, but God can do things that are not humanly possible. The good news is we don't have to understand everything to follow God and be saved from a life of sin. We don't need all the answers to step toward Jesus and choose to believe.

"Because if you confess with your mouth that Jesus is Lord and believe in your heart that God raised him from the dead, you will be saved."
Romans 10:9

Someone trustworthy has a track record of following through on what they say they will do. They keep their promises. Let's take a moment to look at God's track record. Out of the hundreds of prophecies in the Bible that have come to pass, including Jesus' birth (Micah 5:2, Matthew 2:1), crucifixion (Psalm 22:16, Luke 23:33, John 20:25-27), death on the cross (Amos 8:9-10, Matthew 27:45), and His appearance to Saul, James, and hundreds of others three days later (Psalm 16:10, Matthew 28:1-10, Acts 2:22-32), every single one has been fulfilled, without error, down to the most intricate detail. God is batting a thousand. Knowing His track record, we can trust that God will keep His promises. Consider this one from (Jeremiah 29:13): *"You will seek me and find me when you seek me with all your heart."* We can trust God's promises of love, protection, forgiveness, strength, wisdom, and guidance. We can trust that He will reveal Himself to us when we earnestly seek Him. We do this by spending time in His Word, engaging in fellowship with other believers, devoting time to knowing Him through prayer, and putting His Word into practice in our everyday lives. We do this by keeping our mind and heart fixed on Him. Instead of asking, Why me, we should ask, What can I learn from this experience? How can I use this as an opportunity to build my character, strengthen my faith, and become more like Christ? Instead of asking, "Where are you, Jesus?" we can move closer to God by prioritizing our time with Him, reading His Word daily, and participating in small groups. God's love is constant and unchanging, so when we feel distant from Him, we are the one who has walked away.

"Come close to God, and he will come close to you. Clean up your lives, sinners, and clear your minds, doubters. Humble yourselves in the Lord's presence…"
James 4:8,10

Instead of asking, "How could You allow this to happen, God?" we can identify what we feel at that moment (e.g., lonely, heartbroken) and pray to God for His comfort. God promises to bind up the wounds of the brokenhearted (Psalm 147:3), comfort us in our tribulation (2 Corinthians 1:3), lighten the load of the burdens we carry (Matthew 11:28-30), and deliver us out of our troubles (Psalm 34:17) if we belong to Him. It all starts by saying "yes" to God. Instead of asking, "What is your will for my life?" and waiting for Him to hand us a detailed 30-year plan, we can seek the Holy Spirit's guidance in our daily life and allow those decisions to determine our path. We can "pray for an open and willing heart" and "surrender to the Spirit's leading with that friend, child, spouse, circumstance, or decision in our lives right now." When we focus on having all the answers, we steal precious time from investing in building our relationship with God and others – the two things in life that matter most. When we focus instead on building those relationships, our time and energy are used to develop the talents and resources God has given us to serve others so that we can leave a legacy that outlives us. When we put our relationship with God first, setting aside our desires to serve Him, we "live by faith" and learn what it means to be faithful, self-disciplined, compassionate, forgiving, humble, and loving.

We truly forgive others by profoundly understanding how Christ has forgiven us. *"Be kind and compassionate to one another, forgiving each other, just as in Christ God forgave you."* (Ephesians 4:32). We can only fully and completely understand what it means to love unconditionally and forgive wholeheartedly when we experience it for ourselves, not just try to practice it on our own. This cannot be done simply by "being a good person" – to do this, we must have faith in Jesus. When we "live by faith" and accept Christ's invitation to follow Him…

- We gain a personal understanding of true forgiveness, selflessness, and unconditional love at the most intimate level possible.
- We learn to emulate the example of someone who was God in the flesh while understanding what it means to die to our flesh and live a life beyond what we are capable of on our own.

- Our lives can become stories of answered prayers, unexpected blessings, renewed perspectives, and new opportunities that would have otherwise never come our way.
- We become recipients of God's mercy, patience, comfort, healing, strength, and love.
- As a reward for our faith, we experience the joy that succeeds our time on Earth and the eternal rewards that He has promised those who choose to follow Him. In addition, we witness the power of God's supernatural activity in our life on Earth and have the privilege of seeing what God will do with us beyond this life.

"And without faith, it is impossible to please God because anyone who comes to him must believe that he exists and that he rewards those who earnestly seek him."
Hebrews 11:6

If you're struggling with doubt today, ask yourself, "Am I willing to hold on to that doubt and risk never having these opportunities?" Isn't it worth letting go of doubt to risk ending up right back where you started and then wondering if something bigger and more significant is on the other side of your fear? You have nothing to lose and everything to gain by accepting Christ's invitation to know Him, follow Him, and be made new by living according to His Word. Some say, "Let your conscience be your guide." Left to our conscience, we often go away from our faith rather than toward it regarding what God wants us to do. He wants us to do what is Biblically sound. Our conscience is not His standard, nor should it be our guide. The best we can do cannot equate to God's standard of righteousness and holiness. If you could find our way to goodness, we'd not need Jesus' death and resurrection. We would not need salvation. Our faith would be worthless. We'd not need the Holy Spirit. But, because of our sinfulness, we need Jesus and the Holy Spirit to guide us. A Native American Christian said this about our conscience: "In my heart, there is an arrowhead with three points to it. If I do wrong, the arrowhead turns and cuts me. If I do too much wrong, I wear out the points, and it doesn't hurt me much. But when the pain is gone, watch out." We should ask only one source for advice—Jesus. The devil can open doors and invite us into his world. Still, when Jesus chooses us, He gives us the tools necessary to thwart the devil no matter how crafty he is.

"Therefore, I tell you, do not be anxious about your life, what you will eat or drink, nor about your body, what you will put on. Is not life more than food and the body more than clothing?"
Matthew 6:25

Notes From Reading:

____

____

____

____

Questions For The Group:

____

____

____

____

Prayer Request for Today:

____

____

____

____

WEEK TWO

Preparing

For Troubles

Day 8

YOUR GUIDE BOOK

"Hear, my son, your father's instruction, and forsake not your mother's teaching, for they are a graceful garland for your head and pendants for your neck."
Proverbs 1:8-9

DAILY PRAYER

Lord Jesus, I have discounted my parents at times in my life. Yet, I knew that I was to honor them and embrace their guidance and teaching I had yet to do. Please give me the strength to go to my parents, show them my appreciation for them, and provide me with patience when I don't agree with some of their opinions on marriage. Help me respect them not because of just who they are but because you told me to do it.

Do you remember the old song you sang as a kid, *B.I.B.L.E, Yes That's The Book For Me?* Sure, you do. It's OK; no one is listening or watching, so go ahead and let it rip. When we forgo reading the Bible, what we're really saying to God is that we're too busy to put in the work to really get to know Him. That we're good with having a distant relationship with Him. That we sure are happy that He's just a prayer away — but please don't ask us to read that boring, huge book. If we view the Bible as a relic with limited application to modern life, *of course* we're not going to value it or want to read it. But if we view the Bible as God intended — His showing us His heart, His plan for mankind, and the sacrificial gift of Jesus that brings us into right standing with Him — we will afford it the respect it is due. *Because when we value God's Word, we will work to grow our knowledge of it.*

The Bible is the single most important Book ever written. It is an eyewitness account of historical events of such magnitude that they have shaped the world in which we live. Without this Book, the Western world, and a good deal of the Eastern world, would be completely different today. The events recorded in this Book are claimed by a significant percentage of all people who have ever lived on this Earth to be the most important events ever recorded in the history of the world. This Book is foundational to everything humankind will ever know or accomplish.

However, the most important thing we must remember is this: "*All Scripture is inspired by God and is useful to teach us what is true and to make us realize what is wrong in our lives. It corrects us when we are wrong and teaches us to do what is right.*" (2 Timothy 3:16) This verse is perhaps the most relevant in the Bible regarding the importance of Scripture in our lives. It tells us that all Scripture is inspired by God, which means that God inspired the authors of the Bible to write each manuscript. Therefore, every central and significant living area can be found in the Bible, as God knows we need his instructions and guidelines for living. Do you wish you had read a "*how-to*" manual about building a great marriage before you got married? How about a "*how-to*" book before having your first child? Today is your lucky day because both are available to you. Some of us have mistakenly purchased children's toys with ominous words printed on the box," *some assembly required.*" If you did this, you likely needed to read the directions as instructed before assembling the product. Most think, "*I can figure this out,*" and plunge in with both feet. However, few finished the assembly without digging out the "*instruction manual*" to find out what went wrong! Like most of life, marriage and parenting should come with the label "*much, much, much assembly required!*" It takes a lifetime of work to put it together the right way. Most plunge in without reading the instruction manual, confident we will figure it out. However, trouble quickly comes, and we frequently need to read or re-read the manufacturer's instructions. Our problems today can be traced to our failure to study and obey God's instructions. Has there been a time in your life when you felt everything was going wrong? A time when it seemed like, no matter what you did, things were going from bad to worse. Sometimes, we buy into the fact that this is just how life should be. Over the years, you have purchased several cars. The first time you owned a nice car, you probably noticed in the glove compartment a small book with instructions on how to get the best, most satisfying, and most extended service from your purchase. In the *"Owners Manual,"* there are sections on the tire size, pressure, rotations, oil changes, oil weight to use, wiper blades, and care for the seat fabric, to name a few. However, even with all this detailed information, we often need help reading the instructions on protecting one of the most expensive investments we will make. From kitchen appliances to garden tools, most products come with instructions that begin with something like, *"Caution: Please. Read this first before using."*

"All Scripture is given by inspiration of God."
2 Timothy 3:16

There was a time when God took clay, or wet dust, and made the first man. Then, God made a companion from his body, the first woman. *"Then God saw everything that He had made, and indeed it was very good."* (Genesis 1:31). God did not just throw these first humans into some wilderness and tell them to fend for themselves. He meticulously made the place just for them and walked and talked with them, teaching them what they needed to know. Ultimately, God decided to find capable men and provide them with what He wanted to be written in His Holy Book. He put together an instruction book, a history book, and a "*how-to-live*" book. Today, we refer to that Book as the Bible. The Word of God was designed to teach us how to make life work. It is undoubtedly more extensive and detailed than your average instruction book. Reading this book should have a warning label: ***"THIS BOOK WILL CHANGE YOUR LIFE*."**

From the very first chapters of the first Book, you'll learn where you came from, why you are here, and where your journey can lead. Then, you'll discover how to make that journey safer and more rewarding while avoiding painful hazards. We are no evolutionary accident because we are the highest handiwork of God in the physical realm. In this remarkable Book, detailed instructions will help you make this little life work while preparing you for an even better eternal life. No other book in the world has sold more copies than God's Word, yet its wealth of information remains untouched and unused by most who own a copy. For example, the Book of Proverbs is a storehouse of guidelines and helpful instructions for avoiding painful problems you will easily stumble into. It is much better to prevent them than to struggle to extricate ourselves after falling into them. This Book of tremendous wisdom states, "S*o a curse without a cause shall not alight.*" (Proverbs 26:2). In other words, there is a cause for every pain and every problem. If you have the correct information, you can avoid the causes of many of those problems and the pain that comes with them.

Most instructions that come with our products include several dos and don'ts. For example, don't over-inflate your tires, change your oil every 5,000 miles, and replace your filters regularly. Following the manufacturer's recommendations will result in fewer problems for the owner, plus additional years of service. On the other hand, not following them will result in shorter product life, more expensive repairs in the long run, and failure to achieve the desired results. The same is also true of the Bible. If we fail to follow the instructions in God's Word, the results can shorten our lives and increase pain and disappointments.

The Bible includes some dos and don'ts that some believe make our lives less enjoyable. The opposite is true. Within its pages are great diverse topics, such as finances, choosing your friends, achieving and maintaining healthy relationships, what to eat and not eat, and the importance of balance and moderation. In addition, the Bible provides practical advice to help you in nearly every aspect of life. Though the Bible's primary message is to lead you to understand the purpose of life, how to grow in Godly character, and receive the gift of eternal life— God wants you to learn how to avoid many of the mistakes that would cause you to suffer in this life. Jesus Christ said, *"I have come that they may have life and have it more abundantly."* This simple statement, known as the Golden Rule, which Jesus passed on to His disciples, can make an enormous difference in our relationships with others. So, likewise, treating others how we want them to treat us can also make a big difference.

"Finally, brethren, whatever things are true, whatever things are noble, whatever things are just, whatever things are pure, whatever things are lovely, whatever things are of good report, if there is any virtue and if there is anything praiseworthy—meditate on these things."
Philippians 4:8

The Bible is truly the most practical Book you will ever read. It contains laws and principles of living that genuinely work. When Jesus Christ was with His disciples, He made a statement that applies to all the Bible teachings: *"If you know these things, blessed are you if you do them."* (John 13:17). He has made sure that we have an instruction manual because He loves us. It grieves Him to see us suffer needlessly. *"For the*

Lord, God is a sun and shield; the Lord will give grace and glory; no good thing will He withhold from those who walk uprightly." (Psalm 84:11). When you are face-to-face with making major life decisions, there is no better counsel than these words found in God's Word: "*Trust in the Lord with all your heart, and lean not on your understanding; in all your ways acknowledge Him, and He shall direct your paths.*" (Proverbs 3:5-6)

There are several essential points in this Scripture. First, we must pray about our decisions and plans before settling on them as a course of action. We could also ask ourselves, what would Christ do, or what would Christ have me do? Another way of acknowledging Him in all our practices and choices is to look into the Bible to see what counsel we can find to help us with specific situations. Just as there are laws that govern and bring order to physical creation, there are laws that help us avoid many of life's pitfalls and self-inflicted pains.

> *"You shall therefore keep His statutes and His commandments ... that it may go well with you and with your children after you and that you may prolong your days in the land."*
> *Deuteronomy 4:40*

They are so important that God encourages parents to teach them to their children early on. "*You shall teach them diligently to your children, and shall talk of them when you sit in your house when you walk by the way when you lie down, and when you rise*" (6:7). Maybe all hospitals should send a Bible home with the parents of every precious little life with the instructions, "Caution: Read this first!" Likewise, everyone who officiates at a wedding should hand the couple a Bible, letting them know that within its pages is information that can guide them to many wonderful years in a close, loving relationship.

Though Satan loves to whisper in our ears that we're messed up and unlovable mistakes, that's not what the Bible says. To read the Bible is to immerse ourselves in stories that show us how God interacted with His people. The stories include wisdom we can learn from today. The story of Samson, for example, teaches us the perils of being hot-tempered and vain. In the story of David and Goliath we learn that it is God's strength, not man's, that should make us quiver in our boots. And after David had an affair with Bathsheba, even going so far as to murder her husband to cover his sin, we learn of the consistency of God's forgiveness and the sweet relief of being reconciled to Him.

It's hard being a person who seeks after God when we live in a secular world. I don't particularly like being considered not very smart and someone who needs a crutch to get through life. But I have to laugh when I hear those labels slung at Christians. Our relationship with Jesus allows us to live with authenticity and consistency. We don't have to play the game of pretending to have it all together, for one thing. And when we are worried about something, we can hand that fear to Him and know that He's working on it. *The Bible, over and over, promises us God's peace when we rely on Him. God is in control!*

As Sean McDowell notes, "*The Bible has shaped western civilization more than any book ever written.* No other book even comes close." So, clearly, a lot of people have found the Bible worth reading over the centuries. But finding the time to read it in our speedy, modern world isn't always easy. We have so much clamoring for our attention, including television and social media. How many of us, for example, have opened Facebook, "just to check for messages," and found ourselves, an hour or two later, still scrolling through our feed? The Bible is our playbook for life. It outlines the plays as we move the ball down the field. Our reading the Bible gives God opportunities to profoundly change us. Turn the pages of this remarkable Book. Read it with an open mind and an open heart. It contains pure truth about God, about life, the nature of humanity, and your own heart. You'll be amazed at what you discover about God and yourself. If God will indeed be your judge before whom you will someday give an account of your life, it certainly behooves you to be aware of who He is and the simple thing He asks of you before that solemn time comes. In essence, this Book will help you to deal with that same event for which we are all destined. But be warned: **you will not be the same.**

Notes From Reading:

Questions For The Group:

Prayer Request for Today:

Day 9

WHEN TEMPTED

"For we do not have a high priest who cannot sympathize with our weaknesses, but one who in every respect has been tempted as we are, yet without sin."
Hebrews 4:15

DAILY PRAYER

I can hardly believe Jesus that you lived on this Earth for over 30 years and never fell into sin. I can barely make it through my morning coffee before my mind has taken me to places I shouldn't go. The fact that you came to Earth to have that experience I am thankful for. Could you help me to be more like you, Jesus? I am grateful for the Holy Spirit, which reminds me of when I often fall in this world. But I am also thankful I am headed to a place without sin.

An old doctor was confronted by a patient who told him he had broken his arm in two places. The doctor replies, "*Well, stay out of those places*!" He may be on to something. We can't regularly put ourselves in the face of temptation and not be affected by it. When we are faced with the problem of temptation, we need to take the good doctor's advice and "*stay out of them places.*"

Jesus was born to a young virgin and grew up in a small village to be a grown man. He started His ministry and was severely persecuted for who He was. When we think back, we often forget that He lived in the same sinful world we live in today. It is easier to think of Jesus as the person seated at God's right hand in Heaven than to think of all the problems and temptations he dealt with while on Earth. But we can always remember that He came as a real man and experienced real temptations. Temptation is the work of the devil to drag us into his world. We must not miss that we are in a war with an enemy who wants to destroy our family and us as we battle temptation. He wants this because he is envious of your relationship with God. Temptation is all around us. It comes in many forms–financial, sexual, position, privileges, etc. Is our heart so deceitful and desperately wicked that we cannot put up a proper guard over temptation, even at our best? How do we deal with temptation? Temptation wants to take control and overtake us. Temptation wants to dominate us.

Years ago, a new accountant was left alone late one night during his first week at the office. On his desk, someone planted an envelope with a large sum of money enclosed within it. He immediately took the money, put it in his briefcase, and went home. When he arrived at work the following day, he entered the boss's office and put the money on the desk. "*Sir, somehow someone left this money on my desk, and I don't know who it was.*" His boss looked at the new employee. "*I put the money there; it was a test. You passed.*" Life offers us these kinds of tests almost every day. This man could have thought, "*Nobody will know,*" and decided to keep the money. He probably had many uses for the money, but he didn't submit to the temptation.

Satan always tailors his temptations to fit us individually. There are different areas of attraction; it could be pride, greed, power, lust, or another issue you have to deal with. Wherever your weakness is, Satan will attack. It is crucial to identify our areas of weakness and build up barriers so Satan can't get to you or your family. The temptation will lead us on a path where we will begin to reject the fundamental foundations of our faith because accepting what the Bible teaches will condemn our wrong behavior. The temptation will draw us away from the fundamentals of our faith because our faith's fundamentals will fly in the face of our disobedience! It will lead to disbelief — false belief and false teaching.

"So then, brothers and sisters, stand firm and hold. Therefore, since such a great cloud of witnesses surrounds us, let us throw off everything that hinders and the sin that so easily entangles. And let us run with perseverance the race marked out for us...."
Hebrews 12:1-2

Paul said, our battle is not against flesh and blood, but against the principalities, powers, rulers of this world, and spiritual forces of darkness in the heavenly realms. Therefore, most of our spiritual struggle is in our minds and hearts. How would you feel about running a marathon inside your home on a treadmill? It sounds like a crazy idea doesn't it. The scenery would never change, and you could focus only on the digital readout that shows the number of miles ahead. Yet, a man from California recently set a new world record running a 26.2-mile marathon on his treadmill indoors. He beat the previous world record by seven minutes. He said when finished, *"The monotony of a treadmill— the idea that you have to stay balanced for almost two-and-a-half hours — is a lot harder. It became claustrophobic."* Some of us know what he is talking about. For years, we have been running on the treadmill of marriage or the same job with not ever-changing scenery. Unfortunately, the weight of the world's demands us to run in place, never moving forward. The writer of Hebrews tells us that life is the real thing. Your race today is the only one that counts; it is time to put aside everything that would slow you down. Lay aside the demands of the world to have the same clothes worn by friends or fellow employees. Lay aside the desire to own or lease a vehicle equivalent to keep up with your friends.

Lay down the idea that you must live in the best neighborhood, send your kids to the most talked-about schools, or go on the best vacation. Forget that your spouse must resemble the models we frequently see in the media. Instead, refrain from being tempted by Satan to put things ahead of God.

A young boy was in his upstairs bedroom, getting dressed. His mother was downstairs in the living room, talking with a friend. He yelled, "*Is this blue shirt clean enough for me to wear?*" Without hesitation, she said, "*no,*" and continued talking. After a while, he came downstairs, buttoning up another shirt. "*Mom, how did you know that shirt wasn't clean without looking at it?*" "*If you had to ask, it wasn't.*" Many times we wonder whether a course of action is right or wrong. We're not quite sure but we do it anyway. If we think it may be incorrect, we should leave it alone until we're sure we are right. The adage "*When in doubt, don't*" is often an excellent course of action for us to follow.

I like Chuck Swindoll's definition of temptation: "*Temptation is the motivation to be bad by being promised something good.*" We all struggle with it. It might be to get wealthy through dishonesty, climb the corporate ladder by stepping on others, or find sexual pleasure by disloyalty to our spouse. James describes the temptation to sin this way:

"Let no one say when he is tempted, 'I am being tempted by God'; for God cannot be tempted by evil, and He does not tempt anyone. But each one is tempted when he is carried away and enticed by his lust. Then when lust has conceived, it gives birth to sin; when sin is accomplished, it brings death."
James 1:13-15

There are four unchangeable truths about temptation:

Temptation is inevitable. We can't escape it. James says, "*Let no one say when if he is tempted*," but rather "*when he is tempted.*" We can't just run from the battlefield to avoid temptation because the battlefield will find us. We can avoid tempting situations, but it will find us sooner or later. All of us will be tempted to sin.

Temptation is never directed by God. God "*cannot be tempted by evil, and He does not tempt anyone.*" Nevertheless, it is human nature to blame God for our temptations and sins. Remember when God talked to Adam after the first man succumbed to temptation and sinned? Adam's response to God was, "*It was the woman . . . whom you gave me.*" Not only does Adam throw his wife under the bus, but He blames God: "*You gave her to me.*" God allows us to be tempted, but He is never the one who directs the temptation.

Temptation is an individual matter. Every person is "*carried away and enticed by his lust.*" Each of us has a different area of weakness that Satan will try to exploit. One person longs for wealth; another has a pattern of dishonesty. Someone else is driven by ego and a desire for recognition. At the same time, another has an innate desire to pass on inappropriate information. The tempter does not waste his time tempting us in areas of strength. He knows what each of us longs for—individual desires and unique lusts—and zooms in on those.

Temptation always follows the same life cycle. It begins when our sinful desire and temptation meet. That's what James means by "*When lust has conceived.*" But after conception, James says the next step is that temptation "*gives birth to sin.*" Temptation in and of itself is not sinful. It's only when we act on the temptation that it gives birth to sin. And "*when sin is accomplished*," it produces the final aspect of the life cycle of temptation. It yields "*death.*" In (1 Corinthians 10:13), Paul reminds followers of Jesus that we are not compelled to fall into temptation and sin because God always provides a way of escape. What are the multiple paths of escape that God has graciously given us? God is not the one who's tempting you, but He is the one who forgives us and graciously gives us gifts so that we might live life and live it to its fullness. We are not to deceive ourselves into thinking that temptation is God's fault because it makes us even more vulnerable to temptation. Instead, we must focus on the reality that God has generously given us perfect gifts to resist temptation.

The first perfect gift from God is the new birth. Paul spoke of the new birth in (2 Corinthians 5:17) when he said, "*Therefore if anyone is in Christ, he is a new creation; old things have passed away, and look, new things have come.*" Before we came to know the Lord Jesus, we had no choice but to sin. We now have a unique capacity for righteousness. It's now possible for us to say no to temptation and yes to God. Too often, when we succumb to temptation, our natural response is that we want to resist, but we can't help ourselves.

The second gift God has given us is the *Word of God*. James said we were given the new birth "*by the word of truth.*" That refers to the good news of Jesus as found in the Bible, that He died for us and rose again. The entire Bible could be characterized as the Word of truth. Psalm 119:11 says about its relationship to temptation: "*I have treasured Your word in my heart so that I may not sin against You.*"

A third perfect gift for resisting temptation is limitations and escape. Although James doesn't mention it specifically, it is an excellent gift for dealing with temptation. In (1 Corinthians 10:13), Paul wrote, "*No temptation has overtaken you except what is common to humanity. God is faithful, and He will not allow you to be tempted beyond what you can, but with the temptation, He will also provide a way of escape so that you can bear it.*" This is an excellent reminder that God is sovereign despite our temptations. He knows how much we can take and determines how much He will allow. Not only that, but God always provides a way to escape temptation. There is never a circumstance in which we have to sin. The Lord always gives an escape path—we must be alert to find it.

The final perfect gift is a picture of the end. It is a reminder of what will be the outcome of temptation. We're told that giving in to temptation leads to death. It's a great reminder when we are tempted that while giving in may give us temporary pleasure, it always yields a deadly lifestyle. But it also reminds us that using God's gifts to say no to temptation makes us *"first fruits."*

Every day, we can read the news about how some famous person has come to ruin by giving in to temptation. Some choose drugs, some sex; some give in to the temptation of ill-gotten money. What never makes the news on Earth are those who use God's perfect gifts to say no to temptation and yes to obedience to God. The good news is that's what makes the headlines in Heaven.

Notes From Reading:

Questions For The Group:

Prayer Request for Today:

Day 10

SATAN IS AGAINST YOU

"Submit yourselves, then, to God. Resist the
devil, and he will flee from you."
James 4:7

DAILY PRAYER

Lord Jesus, help us recognize when Satan enters our and our family's lives. We were created to be protectors, but evil seems to come from everywhere—our kids' schools, television, media, and kids' games. Lord, help us to learn how to protect our families from evil. I feel overpowered by this task, but I know you can and will help if I ask. I love you, Jesus; help me.

You may have heard the famous country music legend Charlie Daniels sing *The Devil Went Down To Georgia*, but we know that the devil is everywhere, not just in Georgia. Do you believe there is a devil? Are we talking about Satan himself? There are Christians who believe in God yet don't believe in Satan. He exists and actively pursues our soul and those of our family members. When you participate in Christian studies like this one, Satan knows you desire to learn more about Jesus. Evil exists everywhere, and some people believe it more today than ever. The devil realized that if he keeps us busy with work and family, we have less time to worship Jesus. When this happens, Satan is winning the battle for our souls. Scripture tells us that we are to guard against evil in every form. Satan wants us to forget about him and enjoy what he has created for us. He's had some big successes recently. When he worked behind the scenes to remove the Bible from our schools, eliminate prayer from public events and soften the hearts of Christians on issues that were once important to them. He is riding high, and it's time for us to stand up against him.

Has our world always been evil? We can hardly believe what we see and hear when we turn on the evening news. Police officers were killed, and citizens stood back, capturing the moments on cellphones to post on social media. Our world seems different than it was only a few short years ago. Do you remember growing up when you played outside for hours? You could ride your bikes, play in the yard, and never worry about anything. Unfortunately, for many communities, this isn't the case anymore. Satan was *"cast down from heaven"* and became the devil we know today. He is the enemy of righteousness and of those who seek to do the will of our Heavenly Father. He is the author of deception and lies, a subtle and practiced deceiver, and he tries to imitate God's work to lead us astray. Satan uses many techniques to tempt us. He places temptations in our way and encourages us to do bad things, although he has no power over us unless we allow it. Satan cannot seduce us with his enticements unless we consent and yield. When Satan succeeds in deceiving us, we become vulnerable to his power. Even though this supernatural being, this fallen angel and the archenemy of God, has remarkable strength in the material and physical realm — his primary way of opposing God and destroying us is not in the physical or material domain but in the mental or moral realm. With the horrific actions currently on our hearts and minds, we wonder how people can do such evil things. Just think of all the terrible events in our world within the past few years. How did the human race get to this point? The devil is cunning and powerful. The Apostle Paul realized this and wrote to the Corinthian church, letting them know that Satan was working overtime in their church. He wanted to encourage them to be vigilant. Satan's advantage is when people are ignorant of his methods. What are some of the tools that he has used to deceive you? His plans include distraction, discouragement, disillusionment, discontentment, discord, and disassociation.

The first recorded words in the Bible from Satan contradict God. He asks Eve, *"Is it true that God said you couldn't eat from any tree in the garden?"* And Eve says, *"Well, not entirely. We can eat from any tree except the one in the middle. That tree, God said, if you touch it, you'll die."* Satan replies, *"Oh, come on; you misheard. He was exaggerating; you won't die! God knows that you'll be more aware like him. And just like him, you'll be able to discern good from evil."* Eve then sees the tree as good, and she eats from it. Not only did she eat it, but she also gave some to Adam, and he ate it. Then they gained awareness and realized they weren't wearing any clothes. They quickly gather up and sew fig leaves and make coverings. His first step is to get us to doubt God's Word. We need to be on guard for Satan and his helpers. He is trying to convince us that receiving is more of a blessing than giving! He'll have us believing that enormous benefits should come down before we send praises! He'll have us feeling that we owe a tenth of what's left of your money after we've spent the rest on other stuff! He'll make you think you should love yourself before you love your neighbor! Satan will use all-inclusive trickery to get us to doubt God's Word! Satan wants us to believe we don't need to go to church every Sunday or praise him for everything we have! We don't have to honor the Lord at all times or keep His commandments; they are just suggestions! Satan wants us to know that we don't have to read the Bible because the preacher will tell you what you need to know! The devil's mission is to get us to doubt God!

A small family-owned grocery chain decided to cover up offensive magazines and tabloids at its checkout stands. The cover-up was necessary because of all the suggestive and tasteless photos on the covers. The new magazine racks installed covered up everything but the magazine's name. Certain publications are created to target our lusts. It is a war against our souls and the souls of our children and grandchildren. War is raging everywhere. Try to watch a movie, and you are bombarded with inappropriate advertisements. What parents say about video games makes us wonder why we allow these to come into our homes. The devil is doing a fantastic job of appealing to our fleshly lusts. How can we defend ourselves against this onslaught of evil? Peter gives us the key to protecting ourselves against Satan.

"Therefore, since Christ suffered for us in the flesh, arm yourselves also with the same mind, for he who has suffered in the flesh has ceased from sin that he no longer should live the rest of his time in the flesh for the lusts of men, but for the will of God. For we had spent enough of our past lifetime doing the will of the Gentiles - when we walked in lewdness, lusts..." We must arm ourselves with the mind of Christ and saturate our lives with Him."
1 Peter 4:1-3

About ten years ago, the local newspaper in Memphis carried a story about a beaver tunneling into a major levee off the Mississippi River. It must have been a slow news day for something like this to make it into the paper; however, nothing could be further from the truth. This particular beaver worked so hard and effectively that it caused a break in the levee on the river's Arkansas side. He drove a breach in the wall that eventually eroded more than 150 feet of the Mississippi River levee system. That breach caused a torrent that flooded hundreds of acres of farmland, ruining crops for many miles. Life can be just like this. When we think we're safe and secure, a small problem or issue often appears. At first, what seemed to be a minor problem slowly grew into something much bigger than you ever expected. Before we know it, all of our well-constructed security is gone. If issues have been attacking your level, it may be time to fortify your foundation. Before your problems even show up, it's time to seek out help from the Holy Spirit for guidance and support.

Dr. Manuel Padaroyal, a Columbian scientist, developed the first vaccine against malaria, which kills 300 million people annually. He made a lot of waves when he announced that he would give the vaccine to the world for free. Some thought he had lost his mind; others believed he was an earthly saint. We face temptations every day. These temptations come from three sources: the world, the flesh, and the devil. The world is a source of evil and corruption, and while it is our temporary home and we must live here, we must not succumb to it. Unfortunately, Christians often become so much like the world that society can find little difference between those who believe in Jesus and those who don't.

The devil tempts us daily just as he tempted Jesus in the wilderness. Satan knows our weaknesses and will suggest sinful things to us, just as he did to Jesus. He desires to make the Kingdom of God look bad. (John 10:10), *"kill, steal, and destroy everything good in your life to make that happen if you let him."* We don't have to listen to Satan. We don't have to obey him. We can defeat him just as Jesus did by quoting the Word of God. Resist the devil, and he will flee from you as the Bible says, *"Submit yourselves, then, to God. Resist the devil, and he will flee from you."* (James 4:7)

Notes From Reading:

Questions For The Group:

Prayer Request for Today:

Day 11

LIFE'S NOT FAIR

"We are afflicted in every way, but not crushed; perplexed, but not driven to despair."
2 Corinthians 4:8

DAILY PRAYER

God, I love you. Life is unfair to me and to some of those I love. I feel pulled in every direction. Please help me remember that you are a fair and just God. As I go through my day, help me realize everything in my life is happening to bring glory to You. Keep me strong, Jesus, and show me how to get glory to you in everything I do. I love you, Jesus.

Life's just not fair! For example, when someone cuts in front of us when driving, or when we miss our flight because someone took up two parking spaces in the parking lot—that's not fair. Our list can get lengthy. Most of us believe life would be better if things were fair. We'd all get the things we worked for or waited our turn for; then life would be great! As lovely as this theory might be, it's not rational because, in actuality, life isn't fair! When we demand life to be honest, when it isn't, we cause ourselves frustration. Sometimes, our irrational belief that the world has to be fair causes us to become angry and, other times, sad or anxious. However, our internal desire for fairness rarely, if ever, succeeds in rectifying an unfair situation. On the contrary, sometimes our input worsens situations because negative emotions make situations more difficult! When we weigh these observations, it is clear our demand for fairness is not helping us.

How do we function when we often don't experience fairness? The impoverished people of Greenland still have a tough life. Often alone, hungry, and cold, much can be learned about their relationship. They work to retain their traditions, especially regarding hunting. Sure, they own televisions and mobile phones, but they also use dog sleds, kayaks, and harpoons instead of speedboats and snow machines. Among their most straightforward traditions is dividing up a successful kill in a fairway. Here's how it works: One hunter divides the meat into two piles, and a second hunter—with his back turned—indicates which pile he wants. This *"blind"* decision motivates the first hunter to divide the spoils as evenly as possible in the interest of fairness. Fairness is culturally universal. Judgments, transactions, and decisions free from discrimination are prized worldwide. So it likely comes as no surprise that we can choose to treat others legally, exploit them, or cheat.

Great poets often sell far fewer copies of their books than less talented crime fiction writers. Our friends are usually overcome with cancer, while the most hardened criminals remain healthy in prison. Less qualified people win the promotion. Some children are born into poverty, while others are born into affluence. The idea that *"life isn't fair"* isn't just some hard-knock philosophy; it is an observation that an element of random luck affects all of us.

Jonah needed help with the concept of what is fair. His story begins when God calls him to go to the city of Nineveh to proclaim God's impending judgment if the people do not repent. Jonah could have been more enthusiastic about this mission. He has no interest in the well-being of the Ninevites; truthfully, he thinks these Ninevites should be wiped off the face of the Earth. When God told him to go to Nineveh, he thought this was a bad idea. Why even give them a warning? Jonah just wanted to wipe them out and be done with them once and for all. To make matters even worse, Jonah was suspicious that God would let them off the hook. So what does Jonah do? He runs off in the opposite direction of Nineveh; he hops on a boat only to be caught in a massive storm. This leads to him being cast overboard, swallowed by a giant fish, and finally spit out on the shores of Nineveh. Who says God doesn't have a sense of humor? From there, Jonah half-heartedly sulks through the great city, mumbling about turning to God, seeking repentance and warning of God's wrath and destruction. Despite his less-than-heartfelt attempt, the people did repent. They poured ashes over themselves and wore sackcloths to signify their repentance. As a result, the city is saved—with little help from Jonah. We can almost hear him say, "*I knew from the beginning that you wouldn't destroy Nineveh. I knew You would only show love and not punish Your enemies.*" Jonah wanted fairness, not mercy. Nowhere in the scriptures does God claim or promise to be fair. An old saying sums this up: "*When we get what we deserve, that is justice. When we don't get what we deserve, that is mercy. When we get what we don't deserve, that is grace.*" Or, to quote

Mick Jagger and the Rolling Stones—*"We can't always get what we want, but sometimes we get what we need."*

"Everyone then who hears these words of mine and does them will be like a wise man who built his house on the rock."
Matthew 7:24

We must be reminded that clinging to our sense of fairness shows we misunderstand God's ways. God's kingdom is not based on what is fair but on what we need. In the end, we don't need justice; we need grace. Do you remember when Jesus was confronted by a group of angry Jews who were displeased with the attention He gave to the Gentiles? They believe Jesus should spend more time with them, God's chosen people, not sinners and backsliders. So what does Jesus do? He tells them a parable about laborers in a vineyard. Remember how workers were hired at different times of the day to bring in the harvest? When the end of the day came, and each worker was paid, the person who worked all day received the same pay as the person who worked for only an hour. The point Jesus is making is that this seems unfair.

In our traditional way of thinking, people should always get what they deserve. Jesus makes it clear this is not the way God operates. God's love extends to everyone regardless of their situation in life, how good or bad, how faithful or unfaithful they have been, or how long they have been church members. The Bible is full of examples of seemingly unfair situations. On another occasion, Jesus watched the rich making a big show of dropping their bags of money into the temple treasury. A bag of cash is a lot of money, and everyone was impressed with their generosity. When Jesus saw a poor widow drop two small coins into the offering bowl, He claimed she had given more than all the others. How unfair is that! You would think that Jesus would praise the big givers.

After all, if everyone only gives two small coins, how would the temple ever be able to pay its bills? What about the feast prepared for the disgraced runaway son when he returned home after wasting all his inheritance? Nothing was given to the son, who had worked hard and faithfully stayed home while his brother was out having a good time. Where is fairness in that? What about the thief on the cross next to Jesus? He had lived his life with total disregard for God and basic human decency. What does Jesus do when the thief makes a last-minute confession? He told him that he was saved and would enjoy life in Paradise.

So what are we to make of all this? These stories are not about some deserving more than others, a farmer who short-changes his hardest workers, or the Ninevites getting off scot-free. In the parable of the vineyard, all the workers had agreed to work for a set wage. Everyone got what had been promised. The problem was that some workers needed to accept that the boss had the right to be generous to whomever he wished. Jesus is trying to convince us that if God were to be fair and pay us according to what we deserve, we would all end up in the dark shadow of the afterlife. In every situation where Jesus interacts with people, He is telling us something about the generosity of God. God is generous, full of grace, and forgiving. Jesus is not about fairness. He is about faithfulness. We are judged not by our standing in the community or our achievements. Our faithfulness judges us. In the Book of Jonah, God was reaching out and teaching Jonah about grace and undeserved mercy. As we read this passage, we see that God's absolute focus in the story is not on Nineveh! God could have sent anyone to deliver his message to them. A person more enthusiastic about mission work would have done a far better job. Certainly, someone who understood God's grace a little better would have been far more effective.

God's mission was to help Jonah understand that his grace is not selective. What God was trying to get through to Jonah and what Jesus is trying to tell us is that God doesn't operate by what is fair or unfair. The story about Jonah finishes with a question from God. God had caused a plant to grow and shelter Jonah from the hot sun, and then it died. That made Jonah even more upset. God comes to him with this concluding sentence. "*You are concerned about a mere bush that grew one day and died the next. Don't you think I should be concerned about the 120,000 people in that city?*" We need to find out how Jonah responded. Did Jonah finally understand God's mercy and grace?

Notes From Reading:

____

____

____

____

Questions For The Group:

____

____

____

Prayer Request for Today:

____

____

____

Day 12

THE RIGHT THING IS ALWAYS RIGHT

"Give careful thought to the paths for your feet and be steadfast in all your ways. Do not turn to the right or the left; keep your foot from evil."
— *Proverbs 4:26-27*

DAILY PRAYER

Lord Jesus, I keep doing the things that I know I am not supposed to do and refusing to do what I know I should be doing. It is easy to get off track and believe where I am going is the right path. Help me look at where I am as a man, husband, and father. Help me determine if I am on your road or have ventured off. Then, Lord, bring me back if I am not where you want me to be.

Why is it that the good and honest thing to do is often a scary task? Standing up to the person who is visibly a bully. Cutting off a friend we know is not healthy for us. Letting someone (like our child) fail hard so they figure out how to do things independently. These are complicated things, so we think, "I*s it worth potentially damaging my relationships or reputation—just to do what's right? It would be much easier to do the selfish thing."* We often ask, *"Why won't God take this desire away from me so I'll stop sinning?"* People want to be free from sexual sin, substance abuse, gluttony, materialism, love for the world, etc. Again, they ask, *"Why do I keep sinning?"* According to Scripture, the answer is simple: we keep disobeying God.

Most of us are very predictable. Our actions show our priorities. We know the difference between right and wrong, and while we attempt to do good, we also are willing to do wrong even though we know better. We can justify our sinful choices with excuses that can even make us feel sorry for ourselves. Most of us know that our sin is simply a choice to give in to our fleshly desires for a moment or two of comfort and pleasure.

"Do not love the world or the things in the world. If anyone loves the world, the love of the Father is not in him. For all that is in the world — the desires of the flesh and the desires of the eyes and pride in possessions — is not from the Father but is from the world."
1 John 2:15-16

Here are some questions found to help identify the culprit of your sinful actions:

- With whom do you surround yourself?
- Are your friends helping you or hurting you?
- How do you spend your free time?
- What do you think about when your mind is free to wander?
- Do you find yourself making excuses for your sinful actions?

When someone says they have made a mistake and have fallen like having an affair (adultery), they probably didn't fall; they dove. They continually nursed their sin until it became something they couldn't control. So likewise, if we commit sexual immorality, we have made dozens of intentional, wrong decisions to get ourselves to that place. The first phone call. The lustful imaginations. The choice of how we dress, how we act, and what to say. With these choices, we must actively deny our conscience, ignore God's Word, and insist on pursuing what we know is wrong.

"Then desire when it has conceived gives birth to sin, and sin when it is fully grown brings forth death."
James 1:15

Do we ever plan to sin? Do we ever think of ways to get away with what we know is wrong in God's eyes? Of course, we all occasionally fall into sin. God is not silent in helping us find a way out of our sins. He is not holding back the answer to us, who are still enslaved to our old nature. God is willing to help if we are eager to ask. But, he says, *"Choose you this day whom you will serve."* God has given us a mirror to see ourselves in truth, but it is up to us to look into it. We must be honest with ourselves regarding what we allow sin to do to ourselves and our family. Jesus said, *"No one who puts his hand to the plow and looks back is fit for the kingdom of God."* God is loving, forgiving, compassionate, redeeming, and all-powerful, but we must choose *"whom"* we will serve. Once and for all, we must let go of the deceptive pleasures of our sin and cling to our new hearts that only God can give. God gives strength in abundance to those who repent and trust in Him.

Paul said, *"I can do everything through Christ who strengthens me."* If we want to stop sinning, we need to stop. God will give us strength, but we have to do the stopping. If we struggle with alcohol, don't drive by the liquor store. If we have a problem with over-eating, don't drive into McDonald's for the "Big and Tasty." We must replace our lusts with love for honoring God with our body. If pornography is your problem, stop your monthly subscription to the publications and Websites you have been visiting. Scripture includes examples of believers who committed terrible sins. But just like them, why do we want to quit sinning when it feels so good? We enjoy living on the edge. Life is short; if we don't live on the edge, are we missing out on all the fun? Are people getting ahead of us because they don't focus on sin or its consequences? Getting off the right path and stumbling along the wrong way is too easy for us, but it often feels good.

When our stress gets high, we usually seek a shortcut to happiness. Doing the right thing is not easy, but it is always right. Peace comes from laying all our problems at the feet of Christ. We often hear that we should take the less traveled path if we want to be successful. However, only one way exists if we desire eternal life; if we get off that path, we are headed for trouble. Trying to do our own thing, be our own person, or chart our course often leads us farther away from Christ. The world today is anything but a perfect place, and the thought of obeying God can sometimes be daunting. Many will do almost anything to get what they want in life. Today, being rich and dishonest is seen as better than being poor and honest. Sometimes, what works the best is doing what we want now and asking for forgiveness later. We know the value of honesty but choose to live otherwise because we receive greater rewards. In short, being deceptive is part of our lives as long as we live in an imperfect world.

"And as for you, brothers, never tire of doing what is right. If anyone does not obey our instruction in this letter, take special note of him. Do not associate with him, so that he may feel ashamed."
2 Thessalonians 3:13-14

We must do what is right, and doing what is right lies squarely on our shoulders. If we know the difference between right and wrong, we know what to do to please the Lord. God makes this personal; the Bible says, *"And as for you, brothers, never tire of doing what is right."* He puts it in our lap. This is similar to what we hear in Joshua, *"...as for me and my household; we will serve the Lord."* (Joshua 24:15)

"Let your hope keep you joyful, be patient in your troubles, and pray at all times."
Romans12:12

Life comes at us fast, and problems hit us until it hurts. When things go wrong, it is not the time to decide if we will be obedient. We can't always choose our circumstances; we can determine how we will respond. Peter and the disciples saw Jesus walk on water, but only Peter was willing to get out of the boat and try to walk on water himself. Peter trusted in Jesus, but when the circumstances changed, and the waves started kicking up, Peter took his focus off Jesus, and he began to sink. When we focus on our problems, we set ourselves up to fail. Peter took his focus off Jesus and instead concentrated on his frightening circumstances. When faced with determining how to act, sometimes the most challenging part is figuring out how to do the right thing. Of course, how we view the right thing, what we think of as the right thing, makes the difference. We may experience conflicting emotions, feel ambivalent about potential choices, or feel strongly for or against specific actions — whether we are convinced that is the right thing to do. Because we have the Holy Spirit living in us, we know the right thing to do. The right thing is always the best.

Notes From Reading:

Questions For The Group:

Prayer Request for Today:

Day 13

STORMS ARE COMING

*"Then the Lord said to Satan, Have you considered my servant Job? No
one on earth likes him; he is blameless and upright, a man who fears
God and shuns evil. And he still maintains his integrity, though you
incited me against him to ruin him without any reason."*
Job 2:3

DAILY PRAYER

*Dear God, please help me to see your power in this world. You have
often turned your head away from us with all the things that are
happening. I sometimes wonder why things happen to me when trying to
be a follower. When I see those gliding through life with what seems to
be few, if any, problems, I often wonder why. Increase my faith so I can
be the Man of God you want me to be.*

Does God care when the storms of life are headed your way? Does He
care when you are overwhelmed with the trials and tribulations of life?
We, even the most committed believers, will face many difficulties.
Some of us will experience worse problems than others, and others will
face more difficulties. We are all subject to temptations and the trials
and sorrows of this life.

"Indeed, all who desire to live godly in Christ Jesus will be persecuted."
2 Timothy 3:12

We will face all kinds of problems and trials: physical health, loss of
jobs, financial, emotional, family, spiritual, and relationships, etc. We

can't live in this life without dealing with storms. (Romans 8:20-23) Whenever something goes wrong, we hear, "Where was God?" People ask this question because they don't understand who God is. Some believe that bad things should never happen to good people, and when it does, that is a sign that either there is no God or the person has fallen off the wagon. We have all wondered why we go through storms; honestly, we usually look for all ways possible to avoid them. Sometimes these storms seem unfair, but Jesus has a plan for each of us. Not only does He have a plan, but He is working on His project today, and we have yet to learn what He is doing.

A question that is often asked, but many times Christians find it difficult to answer, is: "Why do trials and problems come to those that love Jesus?" We know what Scripture says, but we don't like the answer. Jesus allows things to happen to humble us, grow us, and for those around us to see Him working in us during our trials. While we may wish this wasn't the case, we should worry when we stop experiencing the storms of life. Whether we like it or not, adversity is part of life. Most of us spend much time studying, reading, and even worrying about overcoming adversity when it happens. Problems, large and small, present themselves to us throughout our lives, and regardless of how sharp, intelligent, or happy-go-lucky we are, we will encounter struggle, challenges, difficulties, and heart-wrenching moments. Here's a good question for us to consider: What are you made of? When push comes to shove, when the rubber meets the road, when the chips are down, what lies at the core of who we are? We find out what we are made of when things go wrong. Since our behaviors on the outside indicate who we are on the inside, only by observing how we behave when things go wrong can others see what we have inside us. Life is a continuous succession of problems. They never end.

No sooner than we get control of one situation when another hits us? Life is "two steps forward and one step back." You couldn't possibly have become the person you are today if you had not had to contend with the storms of life. What Do You Believe God Wants You To Be Doing? It is effortless to get caught up in the self-pity, unfairness of life, or "why me?" traps. When we do, we fail to recognize the opportunities for wisdom and growth accompanying adversity. When storms come, the questions begin, and emotions are expressed. Explanations are as plentiful as the amateur philosophers attempting to make sense of things. The "why" questions can often be the most troubling. People ask, "Why did this happen?" Others want to know, "Why didn't God prevent this from happening?" Still, others say, "Why does God allow people to suffer?"

Paul gives an interpretation of the events he experienced after leaving Philippi. Reading Scripture, we discover he is more concerned about the Lord's work than himself. He is in prison and is soon to face a horrible trial. He includes a detailed description of his terrible conditions and his thoughts during his time in prison. Paul rose above any anxiety about death and his prison confinement and suffering. The driving passion of his life made everything else, even imprisonment and possible death, seem insignificant. When he was in prison, what if he had written: *"Here I am in prison, a defeated man. After I have given my life for the cause of Christ, look at what it has brought me. Those that I thought were my friends who should care about me are taking advantage of the situation and using this as an occasion to further themselves. You ought to see the conditions, bonds, and suffering I endure. It looks like I could be executed for my faith. I see little or no hope of release. Things as so bad that not even God can help me now."*

Sometimes the Bible puzzles me. For instance, the book of James starts by telling us that when tough things happen, *"Consider it an opportunity for great joy."* This is a teaching that is hard for many to understand. How does a verse like this apply when we lose someone close and dear to us? Our hearts ache with unimaginable pain when we lose that particular person. The pain we feel and see in our family's eyes is unbearable. When we lose someone to death, does the Bible tell us to quit hurting and be happy? Thankfully, it doesn't. Our natural response when someone dies is to grieve. If you recall, Jesus mourned the loss of His dear friend Lazarus, so I know He expects us to do the same.

A heartbreaking story on the cover of a national newspaper had everyone in our community talking. A groom was found dead only hours after his wedding dinner. One of his friends said, "He was very cheerful and had just gotten married. Nobody could believe he was dead just hours after celebrating his wedding." What we often don't want to hear is that we are just a heartbeat away from eternity.

> *"Our days on earth are like a passing shadow, gone so soon*
> *without a trace."*
> *1 Chronicle 29:15*

However, it usually takes a storm to drive home the reality of our frailty. Therefore, we must be careful about speaking arrogantly regarding our future because we need more understanding of what lies ahead and take charge of it. As believers in Christ, we know that we are not the master of our destiny, for we don't even know what tomorrow will bring (James 4:14). Our lives are so short—here today, gone tomorrow. How should we live in light of these truths? The storms of this life will ultimately lead to joy if we patiently trust in God's plan and discover how to use adversity to grow stronger. How we respond to trials will significantly affect whether they become roadblocks or expressways to learning and growth. When we anguish over difficulties, the experiences only weigh us down. But remembering that these storms are part of the grand plan of happiness can help us see them as opportunities to grow and learn.

Many storms come as a direct result of our actions. For example, when we disregard God's commandments, we follow Satan's plan of misery rather than happiness. Other storms come as a result of unwise choices. For example, many people are burdened with financial debt because they choose to make purchases on credit rather than delay purchases until they can afford to pay in cash. Yet other storms come as a natural result of mortality and our world. We often try to assign fault for every situation. We judge ourselves harshly, concluding that problems occur because of something we did wrong or failed to do something to prevent them. Instead, we should accept responsibility for problems caused by our sins by repenting and continually striving to do better. Storms, however, will come to us regardless of any conscious action on our part. If we blame ourselves for things that are not our fault, we make a bad situation worse by seeing ourselves as bad people who deserve bad things. Storms give us opportunities to show ourselves that we can be faithful. We can choose to feel sorry for ourselves and ask, "Why me?" or we can grow from our trials, increase our faith in the Lord, and ask, "How can I be faithful in the midst of this trial?" We can let adversity break us down and make us bitter, or we can let it refine and make us stronger. We can allow trouble to lead us to drift away from the things that matter most, or we can use it as a stepping-stone to grow closer to things of eternal worth. Spiritual growth can often be achieved more readily by the storms of life than by comfort and tranquility.

One of the purposes of storms is to help us come to know Christ and understand His teachings. When we turn to Christ, we will not only find the comfort we seek, but in so doing, we will also gain an increased testimony of the Holy Spirit, which can heal all suffering. God lets us have difficult days, months, or lives so we can grow from these experiences.

A young woman fought a battle with breast cancer. Although she endured pains and heartache that few people understood, she remained cheerful and optimistic. She wrote her obituary, which, in part, reads: "Today, at the young age of 33, I left this mortal existence to a better place. I was born to wonderful parents who taught me to live life well. We have three sweet children who I will miss greatly. At the young age of 29, I was introduced to something called cancer. Cancer was my great adversary, but I have learned that in this life, our enemies can become our choicest friends; the secret is in learning what to do with the conflict." We live in a world of instant gratification. We want fast food, quick loans, and instant solutions to our problems. However, the Lord may ask us to show our faith by enduring some issues patiently. Today, we may not be able to grasp all the reasons for our challenges or the opportunities they will give us to grow.

"Even when I walk through the darkest valley, I will not be afraid, for you are close beside me." Psalm 23:4

In this very moment, you may be going through a significant storm, where adversities are doing all they can to shake you up and separate you from your faith. Stand on the promises of God. Declare that God's Word is absolute. Let the adversities know they can shake the circumstances around you, but they can never shake the faith within you. Stay rooted and be assured that Jesus will bring you out of this situation with a testimony of victory. God is using everything for good and His glory.

Notes From Reading:

____

____

____

____

Questions For The Group:

____

____

____

Prayer Request for Today:

____

____

____

Day 14

KEEPING YOUR WORD

"The Lord detests lying lips but delights in trustworthy people."
Proverbs12:22

DAILY PRAYER

Dear God, search me today. Help me see myself the way You see me concerning being a truthful man. Lord, help me focus this week on becoming a man of integrity through my Word. Help me be someone that does what I say. Search me and draw out what you want me to learn. Help me to become the man you desire me to be.

Few things define a person more than whether or not they can be trusted. A truthful and honest person in their daily dealings shows a glimpse of their Heavenly Father. Unfortunately, even the most genuine people are capable of deception. Deception refers to the act—big or small, cruel or kind—of causing someone to believe something untrue. Various studies have revealed that the average person is less than real several times daily. Therefore, men and women of God must strive to be honest and truthful in all dealings. Although some say it doesn't, it should matter what people think of you. We have given up our old selves to be a follower of Jesus Christ, so when people observe how we speak, act, and behave, they may decide if they want to have a relationship with Christ. So what would people say about your consistency, to always be truthful? Sometimes, always, or never? What Bothers You About People That Are Not Truthful? There is a cost to being untruthful. Those who lie and get caught being untruthful often find it challenging to win their way back to being trusted again. Interestingly, in our culture of a lack of honesty, it is still one of the worst things you can say of someone..."You are a liar." Of course, almost everybody distorts the truth, but no one wants to be labeled a liar.

"Do not lie to one another, seeing that you have put off the old self with its practices and have put on the new self, which is being renewed in knowledge after the image of its creator."
Colossians 3:9-10

The book The Day America Told the Truth reports that:
    91 percent routinely about matters they consider trivial
    36 percent lie about important issues
    86 percent regularly lie to parents
    75 percent to friends
    73 percent of siblings
    69 percent of spouses

The world recognizes that for a wide variety of practical reasons, we need to be able to trust what people tell us. However, when people don't tell the truth, havoc reigns in society, our work, our families, and our relationships; it can have serious consequences when we don't tell the truth. Did you ever stop to think how much of our world can be hurt by lies? We've seen it in the leadership of major corporations that are not truthful about their companies' financial picture and have caused millions of dollars to be lost in the stock market, resulting in thousands of people losing their life savings. Not being truthful is contagious. First, we start with "little lies, or white lies." It can then grow to more consequential severe lies. Then, the more it seems acceptable, the more it becomes routine. If you feel like everyone needs to tell the truth, it doesn't seem wise to go out of your way to be honest. Some would say you're just shooting yourself in the foot if you don't lie; the cheaters get ahead. Do you think appealing to fairness is enough to make people tell the truth? More than appealing to fairness is needed. Without a stronger foundation than that, we breed more untruthfulness. What it takes is a fundamental change. It takes a change of heart.

"Do your best to present yourself to God as one approved, a worker who does not need to be ashamed, rightly handling the word of truth."
2 Timothy 2:15

Our worth comes from Christ and not from ourselves, so we don't need to pretend to be better than we are; we don't need to put on a mask. We are flawed, and those around us already know this. What freedom not to have to prove anything! What a relief! Yet, we still don't tell the truth. We fudge when we fail to recognize our weaknesses, failures, struggles, and defeats. We sidestep the fact when we pretend to know God better than we do. We are dishonest when we attempt to give any false impression that we are outstanding prayer warriors, greatly devoted to Christ, or brimming over with love and compassion when the truth is otherwise. In short, we are not truthful when we engage in hypocrisy to deceive others, whether concealing our sins or exaggerating our accomplishments. And the greatest danger in this kind of deception is that we will end up deceiving ourselves. As the author Nathaniel Hawthorne wrote: "No man, for any considerable period, can wear one face to himself and another to the multitude, without finally getting bewildered as to which one is true." In other words, if we are continually trying to convince others that we are better than we are, we may start to believe it. Walking with Christ requires an ongoing habit of repentance and a frank acknowledgment of our sins. Without that, we soon become proud. Integrity is honesty in action. One of the popular sports where no visible referee or umpire is watching over the athlete's shoulder is golf. During a tournament, there are course officials on the course. If a player touches the ball and it moves, he should count it as a stroke even if no one sees the ball move. Golf is unique in that the players will self-report themselves when a rule has been broken. This integrity is an integral part of the game.

Boaz was an honest man. His honesty is a Godly trait, and his honesty is straightforward. People knew where they stood with him, and he said what needed to be said, and he did it with kindness. Using half-truths, Boaz could have married Ruth and gained a wife and an inheritance. Still, he knew a closer family member who should have had the opportunity first. He and Ruth had already spent time talking together during the harvest. He had already protected her during the harvest and admired her relationship with Naomi, her mother-in-law. Boaz did not try to "finagle" to make Ruth his responsibility. Half-truths are lies... and are cover-ups for the truth. In the day of "fake news" and "alternative facts," we need the truth. We live in a time when if it is on the internet, written in the newspaper, or seen on the evening news, we believe it is true. We repost articles from our favorite news sites, never considering whether the slanted message or partial view is factual. In doing so, we do the opposite of what we are called to do—spread the truth. God doesn't want us to apply what is false. He calls us to spread the truth. We should realize there is no difference between gossiping behind a friend or acquaintance's back and spreading false news on any social media platform. The Lord detests a lying tongue, no matter where the lie originated. We are called not to walk, live, and speak from a place of virtual reality... fake news... alternative facts but from the truth that God has given us.

This quote was in an article about high school students cheating: "What's important is getting ahead," said one student. "The better grades you have, the better college you get into, and therefore, the better you'll do in life. If you learn to cut corners, you'll save time and energy. The better you do, that's matters. It's not how moral you were in getting there." Students think it's unfair that they must study to get a good grade, so they cheat. Others believe that music companies make too much money, so they download illegal songs. One writer said: "For working stiffs, stealing office supplies and padding expenses feel like petty acts of revenge against a system in which rich people wangle their way out of their proper share of the tax burden, and corrupt CEO's get away with rap-on-the- knuckle fines." Some say that lying is associated with excellent social skills. Social skills are needed to control your words and what you say. Is convincing lying associated with good social skills? "You look nice today." "Love that dress. Have you lost weight?" "Your hair is unbelievable." "Your kid is a one-of-a-kind great athlete." "You are so beautiful inside." "I wish I could spend more time with you." Study after study shows that lying is a way of life for many. The more people do it, the more it becomes accepted. And the more people accept it; the more people do it.

"Those who want to get rich fall into temptation, a trap, and many foolish and harmful desires that plunge people into ruin and destruction. For the love of money is the root of all kinds of evil. Some people, eager for money, have wandered from the faith and pierced themselves with many griefs."
1 Timothy 6:9-10

Our verse today is perhaps one of the most misquoted texts in the Bible, and it has been used to degrade many wealthy people. Money is not the root of all evil; the love of money is the root of all evil. The love of money and devotion to getting more and more money will drive people to all kinds of evil.

Over the centuries, some whoppers of excuses have been told to God. Moses comes to mind. Both Moses and Jonah had a good reason. But, of course, that did not keep Jonah out of the belly of the great fish! Being untruthful and making excuses for not wanting to do what God wants is an insult. God knows what is in your heart coming out of your mouth before you speak it.

Notes From Reading:

Questions For The Group:

Prayer Request for Today:

WEEK THREE

Living In The World, But Not Of The World

Day 15

WHO DO YOU WORK FOR?

"Whatever you do, work heartily, as for the Lord and not for men, knowing that you will receive the inheritance as your reward from the Lord. You are serving the Lord Christ."
Colossians 3:23-24

DAILY PRAYER

Dear Jesus, help me use my work to let others see you. Place me in places where you want me to show others what it means to work for You. Please help me be honest in my dealings and control my actions to show others that I have a much more critical boss than anyone in our organization.

We are often defined by what our occupation is. The question is, "What do you do for a living?" That is an exciting way to find out the information we seek. They ask, "What do you have to do every day so that you can live?" For many of us, we didn't necessarily choose our employment path. It chose us out of our necessity to live. Most of us have a job that focuses on pleasing a boss or a group of bosses. The politics and pressures in the job market today can be overwhelming, and working to please a boss can often put us in an uncomfortable position. We were created to work, and it is part of God's plan that we work. It doesn't matter what we do or where we work; our work is where God can use us to influence our society. Work is often not where we think about making a significant difference for Jesus; however, it can be where we can show co-workers that God cares and wants to be involved in their lives. To work means we're productive members of society, and our work can frequently be a sense of pride. Our work can even be a place where we worship; however, our work's most significant focus is often—pleasing our boss. The question is, who is your boss? Work gives us structure and defines us as functioning, contributing, and worthwhile citizens. It makes us part of a community of fellow workers. The person who loves work will likely be happy and content, but the danger is close when we become more tied to our work than our faith and family. Becoming a workaholic can be very unhealthy and poison us from the people we feel closest to. Our family must recognize our hard work and why we work so hard. What would happen tomorrow if you arrived at work and Jesus Christ stood there as your boss? Well, after someone picked you up off the floor, would Him being your boss make a difference in your attitude, appearance, or mood?

"Whatever you do, work at it with all your heart, as working for the Lord, not for men." Colossians 3:23

We should do our best, remembering that the ultimate boss we are serving is Jesus Christ. Whether raising a family or working out of the home, if we perform our Job as if Jesus is our boss, we will do it "with all our hearts." When someone approaches a job with apathy or indifference, we call it "a half-hearted effort." When we do something with all our heart, it means we are enthusiastic about it. When we are passionate, we bring glory to God in our work. If we are doing our Job for the approval of Jesus, we will always do more than the bare minimum. In Jesus' time, the Jews were under the domination of the Roman Empire. A Roman soldier had the legal authority to demand that any Jew carry his equipment for exactly one mile. The Jews hated to do this, and they bitterly counted each step. Finally, at exactly one mile, they dropped the load and said disgustingly, *"There! I've done what is required!"* But Jesus requires a higher standard for His followers. He said, "*If someone forces you to go one mile, go with him two miles.*" (Matthew 5:41). A Roman soldier would not soon forget the person who cheerfully carried his equipment the second mile. Are you a one-mile worker in your current Job? Do you do only the bare minimum of what is expected so as not to lose your position? Or do you go the second mile and leave the mark of excellence in your work? People will never forget second-mile-workers.

"Do not conform to the pattern of this world, but be transformed by the renewing of your mind. Then you can test and approve God's will—his good, pleasing, and perfect will."
Romans 12:2

God does not want us always to play it safe. The life of a Christian should be an adventure. The journey with God is full of surprises; we never know what is around the next bend. We never know when we will have the opportunity to change someone's life through our actions. One of the most important decisions of our lives will require us to stop being like everyone else and stand out as someone different, both at work and in the community. We must always appreciate the importance of one moment, Word, and deed in someone's life. These moments seldom come at a convenient time and will never come if we stand on the sidelines. Instead, we can seize the moment to give of ourselves or walk on the other side of the road, as we learned in the good Samaritan parable. Capturing the moment is stepping up and allowing God to step in. People are watching you at work to see if you tell the truth, act how you say is meaningful, and say what you mean. Scripture tells us to refrain from saying anything we don't mean.

We make things worse with our non-Christian brothers and sisters at
work when we lay down a smoke screen of pious talk saying, "I'll pray
for you," and never do it. Or saying, "God be with you," and not
meaning it. Jesus calls us to develop a reputation so committed to
integrity that we never have to preface anything we say with an oath or a
statement that says this is true. Our lifestyle and our testimony are such
that whatever we say is true.

As a moral philosopher wrote, "It is easy to tell a lie, but it's hard to tell
only one." When we see ourselves shading the truth and not being
honest, we must stop and think: this probably won't hurt anyone right
now, but the untruthfulness will harm my relationship with Christ. We
can never have deep relationships without being a person of our Word.
When someone says they will do something or commit to something and
continually fail to keep their Word, they soon lose all respect for you
and who you belong to. At work, people need to believe they can trust
your Word. People must trust that if you say something, you mean it; if
you commit, you will do it; and if you say you will be there, you will.
Everyone works. Some get paid to work, while others do some work
where you don't receive money for your tireless efforts. If you are
raising a family, that indeed works. You may not participate in paid
employment, but if you are in the business of growing your family, you

are a rock star. How do you view work? Where would you place it if you classify work somewhere between absolute pain and misery and it is the best thing in the world to which you can aspire? Many consider work a struggle—whether it's the work you get paid for or housework. Some may see paid work in terms of money. Simply a way of purchasing a lifestyle you'd like to become accustomed to. Work also may be a way to satisfy your ego and receive recognition. Finally, many see work as a way to use and develop skills or accomplish something meaningful.

God's instructions to us in (Genesis 1) is, *"Be fruitful and increase in number; fill the earth and subdue it. Rule over the fish of the sea and the birds of the air, and every living creature that moves on the ground."* Then God said, *"I give you every seed-bearing plant on the face of the whole earth and every tree with fruit with seed in it. They will be yours for food."* So work was ordained at creation. Everyone knows that workers need the right tools. Jesus' father, Joseph, was a carpenter, and Matthew called him *"a righteous man."* But we need to consider the wisdom he handed to Jesus concerning work. Wisdom like:

Measure twice, cut once
Use the right tool for the Job.
Take care of your tools, and they'll take care of you.

In ancient times, it was customary for a son to follow his father into his trade. Joseph practiced his trade in the small village of Nazareth, but he probably worked in nearby towns. Recent archaeological digs about four miles from Nazareth have shown that extensive building was constructed during the years that Joseph would have worked as a carpenter. Much later in Jesus' life, when he returned to his hometown of Nazareth to teach the Gospel, the people in the synagogue couldn't get past his former life. As a carpenter, Jesus must have learned many lessons about the woodworking trade from Joseph.

A story about the infamous Dr. Howard Hendricks from the Dallas Theological Seminary has been told. He was on an airliner that was delayed on the ground, and several passengers grew increasingly impatient. One obnoxious man kept venting his frustrations on the stewardess. She responded graciously and courteously despite his abuse. After they finally got airborne and things calmed down, Dr. Hendricks called the woman aside and said, "I want to get your name so that I can write a letter of commendation to your employer." He was surprised when she responded, "Thank you, sir, but I don't work for American Airlines." He sputtered, "You don't?" "No," she explained, "I work for my Lord Jesus Christ." She explained that before each flight, she and her husband would pray that she would be a good representative of Christ on her Job. She sought to please God first.

Notes From Reading:

Questions For The Group:

Prayer Request for Today:

Day 16

FINDING BALANCE

*"The Lord God took the man and put him in the Garden of Eden to work
it and take care of it."*
— Genesis 2:15

DAILY PRAYER

*Jesus, you know what a battle I am having with balancing my life right
now. I sometimes feel as though my job is my life. I know I am
commanded to work and provide for my family, but I often get out of
balance. My family has now grown accustomed to the money I make
working long hours, and I can't seem to stop. Please help me balance my
life and place You at the very center.*

How often do we hear this expression, "We must do all things in balance
and moderation." What does that mean when you listen to it? It certainly
sounds like the responsible thing to do! Surely we should "order our
lives" in a way that pleases the Lord. Yet, though this might sound
prudent and wise, beneath the facade of responsibility and good
judgment, too often lies an ancient and evil desire. We are not against
order and balance. On the contrary, we thank God for the glorious
balance that we see all around us in His creation--a balance beyond the
power of mere men to effect. The problem with the balanced Christian
life is that it is also often beyond our control. God called us from the
beginning to work but never to make work our God. He ensured we
knew we would provide for our direct and extended family. However,
working has changed for all of us and has become more than a means to
live but, in some instances, who we are. The average workweek at one

time was forty hours. A recent national poll put the average number at forty- seven hours per week, or 9.4 hours per day, with many saying they work fifty hours per week. Being on the job these many hours means we often spend more time at work than with our families. The world wants you to believe that your existence should revolve around work and your children's and grandchildren's extracurricular activities. After all, it is the world that is currently defining success. The more we work, the more things we are involved in determining your success. We often brag about how much pressure we are under at work, how much work we have to take home, and the frustrations of keeping up with all the extracurricular activities. The pressure on us today is overwhelming. We work hard, not because we want to be away from our families but because we want to provide for our families. We want our children to have an excellent education, the desired toys, a safe and comfortable home, and reliable transportation. We like seeing our children's faces when we can take them on vacations or buy them things they desire. Isn't that why most of us work so hard?

If we work less than 50-plus hours, attend events four nights a week, and always be available on our cell phones, then we aren't interested in our life or career. Of course, some jobs require such an effort, but we might ask ourselves if we allow our work to become more important than our spouse, children, and most of all, Jesus. It's our time and energy; if we spend all our time and energy at work, who gets what is left over? What do our schedules say about the balance we claim is essential? We are developing an unholy relationship between work and everything we pack into our schedule. Scripture teaches us that if we focus on Kingdom work, we will make all our work meaningful. If we focus on using all we do for Kingdom purposes, our daily work will have power and joy rather than struggle and despair. *"What does man gain by all the toil at which he toils under the sun?"* (1:3). *"What we*

buy with the money we earn doesn't last. Still, work is a gift from God."
(2:24) But like all of God's blessings, work is often distorted.

It is challenging to balance living in the secular world and thriving in
our spiritual lives. Can we be good Christians and be successful in our
careers at the same time? Is it possible to realize our full potential in our
profession and still have a healthy play and rest balance? The world is
more advanced and efficient than in the past. Yet, it is ironic that we are
often much busier and suffer more stress than ever. Greater efficiency
but less time—how can we strike a balance between our career, family,
and spiritual life becomes a matter that requires a real thought-out
strategy. Many tackle this challenge by breaking their lives into phases
and focusing on one area at each stage. But, unfortunately, our
prioritization process is also often quick to rank career first, family
second, and our faith journey a distant third. Hence, striking a balance
here usually means that "God can wait" or "We will make up time for
the family later."

In the parable of the wedding feast, the king ordered his servants to call
those invited to attend the banquet. Still, the invitation was taken lightly
as each was busy. The king was furious and deemed those invited
unworthy (Matthew 22:2-8).On another occasion, Jesus called someone
to follow Him. Although the response seemed optimistic on the surface,
the person asked Jesus to wait as he had first bid farewell to his family.
Jesus deemed this man unfit for the kingdom of God. (Luke 9:61-62)
These two passages remind us that putting off God's matters to a later
date to focus on our career or our family may not be a wise choice.

"Do not overwork to be rich; because of your understanding, cease!
Will you set your eyes on that which is not?"
Proverbs 23:4, 5

Effective managing our time and energy starts with realizing that it is not about focusing on different aspects at different phases of our lives. A successful balance also does not pivot on equal time allocation. The only way to achieve a balance is to make Jesus the pivot and balance everything around Him. This means that our sole focus is God and nothing else! This does not suggest that Christians are irresponsible workers in society and negligent spouses or parents at home. The motivation to do an excellent job at work is not our relentless and blind pursuit of material rewards, career advancement, or the satisfaction of our ego, but rather the natural need for a good Christian to do the right thing, be an example, and bring glory to the name of God. A person who loves God and walks near Him will know how to care for their family and rely on Him to build a strong, loving family. As we draw closer to God, He will give us the wisdom to naturally strike a balance in faith, career, and family. Therefore, focusing on God is the formula for managing conflicting demands for our time and energy.

Christians seeking to serve God may face the dilemma of whether they should allow the fullest potential in their career to be realized. The corporate world always pushes for better performance year after year. It seeks to promote performers to achieve higher responsibility levels. The question is whether Christians should continue to attain or accept more and more senior positions in their careers, which often compromises the time for and the quality of service to the Lord. On the other hand, are Christians meant to be underachievers even if they may not necessarily be under-performers? On the contrary, the Bible desires Christians to be achievers.

There are examples of God's people who attained very high levels of achievement. At only thirty years of age, Joseph became second only to Egypt's Pharaoh, a leading nation then. (Genesis 41:40-46) Daniel became one of three governors under King Darius. (Daniel 6:1, 2) However, one commonality in these cases is that the achievements were unequivocally the work of God to fulfill His unique purpose. Neither Joseph nor Daniel actively sought their high-ranking position. All they did was continue their faith and integrity toward God, even in adversity. When tempted, Joseph did not yield to his mistress and, when jailed, did not murmur against God (Genesis 39:7-20). Daniel did not compromise his beliefs to enjoy Babylon's delicacies and risked his life to continue to pray three times a day, as was his custom (Daniel 6:1-10). They did the right thing. God paved the rest of the road to achievement.

While everyone's situation is unique, maintaining a close relationship with God, devoting ourselves to prayer, and consistently seeking wisdom from Scripture should undoubtedly provide solutions to whatever circumstances we face.

Let us picture the scene at our retirement party. On that day, we are surrounded by colleagues and business associates celebrating your illustrious career. What thoughts will be racing through your mind? What will you rejoice over? What will be your regrets? Will your family still be there, rejoicing and celebrating with you? Will you take comfort in knowing you have been a light to the world and salt to the earth? Will you be thankful that God has walked with you and guided you through your entire career? Will God be pleased with you?

Notes From Reading:

____

____

____

____

Questions For The Group:

____

____

____

Prayer Request for Today:

____

____

____

Day 17

IMPORTANCE OF FAMILY

"Do not be conformed to this world, but be transformed by the renewal of your mind, that by testing you may discern what the will of God is, what is good and acceptable and perfect."
—*Romans 12:2*

DAILY PRAYER

God, I love you. I am so busy. I feel pulled in every direction. Please help me focus on the one thing you call me to do—Bring glory to You. As I go through my day, help me realize everything I do that brings glory to You is my purpose. Show me, Lord, how to give credit to you in everything I do. I love you, Jesus.

If pop culture is any indicator, today's family has strayed far from the days of "Leave it to Beaver." Ward and June Cleaver, the idyllic suburban parents of the mid-20th century, has been replaced by characters like "Modern Family's" Jay Pritchett, a patriarch who remarried a woman closer in age to his grown children than himself. The Cleavers and their two sons represent the small nuclear family of the '50s and '60s; the Pritchetts portray present-day family dynamics' complexity. While Pritchett's character particularly values tradition, his Colombian trophy wife and children carry the show into the 21st century. Just take Pritchett's son Mitchell, who is raising his adopted Vietnamese daughter with his partner, Cam.

The infamous Zig Ziegler loved golf and once took his son to the golf course. His son was still relatively new to the game, but Zig was impressed by his performance on one of the par-four holes. At the tee, the boy lifted the ball straight and true down the fairway. A second shot got him onto the green within 14 feet of the cup. Wanting his son to succeed, he went to great trouble in sighting the shot for him and gauging the putt's lie and then told his son just how he ought to play it. His son stepped up to the ball and put the ball perfectly into the cup just as his father had taught him—his first birdie. Then it was Zig's turn. He also had made the green in two shots, but his putt was far more manageable. For a moment, he considered flubbing the shot so that he would not overshadow his son's achievement. Still, he decided against it because it would go against everything he had taught his son about doing his best. Instead, he sank the putt quickly and also birdied the hole. As they walked to the next tee, Zig casually asked his son, "Well, son, were you rooting for me on that last shot." "Dad," the boy replied, "I always root for you." "I always root for you"—that's the kind of commitment we desire in our families. It's a commitment that we always will seek the best for our spouse, children, friends, and parents. It constantly seeks a way to help them grow and succeed—always wanting them to get ahead and win. And that's the kind of commitment God wants for His family too.

In Deuteronomy 6, God says to Israel: If you want your families to succeed in life--if you're genuinely committed to your household, then here's what you have to do: "Love the Lord your God with all your heart and with all your soul and with all your strength. These commandments that I give you today are to be upon your hearts. Impress them on your children. Talk about them when you sit at home and when you walk along the road, when you lie down, and when you get up. Tie them as symbols on your hands and bind them on your foreheads. Write them on the doorframes of your houses and your gates." If you ask most men or women what the essential thing in their lives is, you will hear, *"my children.*" The Bible does not teach that we should put our family first! Jesus, Himself, taught us that we dare not do that. In (Matthew 10:37), Jesus said: "*Anyone who loves his father or mother more than me is not worthy of me; anyone who loves his son or daughter more than me is not worthy of me.*" We will only have the kind of family we want if we commit to God first. God knows who we are committed to and will determine who sets the rules. If you are committed to your family first, you won't obey God if they're unhappy. For example, there was a family where little Johnny couldn't do anything wrong. And being a precocious little boy, little Johnny would periodically misbehave in Sunday School. One day when he was corrected for misbehaving in Sunday School, the parents didn't talk to the teacher to find out what had happened (she had acted properly, by the way). They didn't bring him back to church. Why? Because little Johnny is their priority, not God. They ended up divorcing themselves from God because little Johnny wasn't happy.

"Commit to the Lord whatever you do, and your plans will succeed."
Proverbs 16:3

If you are committed to your family first, you will do what we (rather than God) think is right. For example, my friend heard a man bragging about the great movies he and his grade school sons had watched together. This man wasn't a Christian, but most people would be appalled at what he allowed into his house. The movies displayed disrespect for authority and were loaded with profanity. While my friend tried to be tactful (because he was trying to win this man to Christ), he noted that he would be worried about bringing that kind of movie filled with cursing into his two kids' house. The man scoffed and replied: "They're going to hear that kind of language eventually; they may as well hear it here in my house with me."To him, this made sense. These were his boys, and he wanted to share the movies he liked to watch with them.

If you put your family first, then sooner or later, God will come second. But when we put God first, our family will benefit because God will set the rules for treating our family. In (1 Peter 3:7), husbands are told to *"be considerate as you live with your wives, and treat them with respect as the weaker partner and as heirs with you of the gracious gift of life, so that nothing will hinder your prayers."* God says that if husbands mistreat their wives, He won't listen. He won't hear their prayers. In (Ephesians 5:33), husbands are told that they "must love his *wife as he loves himself, and the wife must respect her husband."* God commands wives to respect their husbands. To not put them down or belittle them. Then in (Ephesians 6:1-3), *"Children, obey your parents in the Lord, for this is right. Honor your father and mothe*r"— the first commandment with a promise— that it may go well with you and you may enjoy long life on the earth." This isn't the same kind of thinking that Bill Cosby displayed when he threatened his kids: "I brought you into this world, and I can take you out!" God tells our kids that they must learn to honor their parents to survive in this world. If they don't, they'll suffer and live lives that won't be what they'd hoped for. And Fathers are told, *"do not exasperate your children; instead, bring them up in the training and instruction of the Lord."* (Ephesians 6:4). Notice that all these are commands from the Lord. We may not always want to do these things. Still, even if we don't want to do them - if God is our priority— if we're committed to pleasing God above all else in life, we'll follow them because this is what God wants.

If we are committed to God, we must understand that we signed our entire life to Him once we became Christians. We don't own anything. We don't own our homes, our car, or even the clothes on our backs. We don't own our wives or husband or our children. They all belong to the Lord, and God tells us that He will hold us accountable for what is now His. He keeps us responsible for treating our spouse or disciplining our children. They are His, not ours.

"Commit your way to the Lord; trust in him, and He will do this: "He will make your righteousness shine like the dawn, the justice of your cause like the noonday sun."
Psalms 37:5-6

In other words: "You put God first… God will put you first." We all want what's best for our family. Sometimes, those who are not Christians will, by instinct, do what God commands us to do as Christians. Perhaps their parents modeled this lifestyle for them. Maybe they've seen Christians who've treated their families Biblically and have copied that. Thus, we all (Christians and non-Christians alike) try to ensure our family is well provided for. We all want our children to:

Have the best education.
The best healthcare
The best opportunities for a good job when they graduate
To marry well
To raise children/grandchildren that we are proud of
To be financially taken care of

One day a small boy tried to lift a heavy stone but couldn't budge it. His father, watching him, finally said, "Are you using all your strength?" "Yes, I am!" cried the boy. "No, you're not," said the father. "You haven't asked me to help you." So what God is saying here is that we must teach our children to ask Him for help. And we will teach them this by helping them to remember that God allowed us in the past. So let's make it a regular part of our lives to remember what God has done for us in the past (when we have faced difficulties and obstacles). Then, we'll be more inclined to look to God for help with problems in life. And if that's true in our lives, then our children will be more willing to look to God when life gets complicated.

Years ago, in Reader's Digest, one young woman told how her dad used to teach God's providence to his children. She said she remembered this story from her youth: Her dad said: "Seems like some of our neighbors expect to be sharecropping forever. But it doesn't have to be that way, now. Look at the boy Joseph there in the Bible." She said then her dad wove the wondrous story about a young man thrown into a dark slimy pit. Then he said: "Joseph didn't stay in that hole. Joseph expected to be a leader, not a forgotten young man at the bottom of a pit. And do you know what happened to him? One day..." and then he told of how God worked in Joseph's life to pull him out of that pit and raise him to be the second most powerful man in Egypt. It was such a powerful lesson that she remembered it even as an adult.

If we believe that God can act in our lives if we're convinced that God has worked, and if we're committed to putting God as the central force in our lives—then our kids and grandkids will pick that up. They'll learn to trust in our heavenly father because they've seen that we have learned to trust in our father. The Bible makes it very clear when it says marriage is the grace of life. Children are a blessed heritage from the Lord, and we must understand the blessedness, the bliss, and the purpose of God that unfolds in marriage and raising children. Family is still the heart and soul of human society and family as God defines it; it is the place of intimacy. It is a place of joy. It is the place of memories that build the foundation of life. It is the place of love. It is a place of socialization. It is the place of morality. It is a place of security.

Notes From Reading:

Questions For The Group:

Prayer Request for Today:

Day 18

DON'T COMPROMISE

"Do not be conformed to this world, but be transformed by the renewal of your mind, that by testing you may discern what the will of God is, what is good and acceptable and perfect."
—Romans 12:2

DAILY PRAYER

God, I love you. I am so busy. I feel pulled in every direction. Please help me focus on the one thing you call me to do—Bring glory to You. As I go through my day, help me realize everything I do that brings glory to You is my purpose. Show me, Lord, how to get glory to you in everything I do. I love you, Jesus.

The Christian life is a spiritual battleground with a hateful and dangerous enemy. (1 Peter 5:8), *"Your adversary the devil"* who prowls to catch us off guard and then devour us. The spiritual battle with Satan begins when we surrender our life to God. He is out to claim our souls and will do anything to get it. Just as there is a living God in Heaven who wants us to do His will, there is a deceiving devil on earth who wants us to move outside of the will of God by a compromise. Satan wants to take as many with him as possible, so he uses deception to have us compromise regarding our faith. The beginning of compromise is the first cut from the vine. It is usually not a complete detachment but a gradual process. For example, moving away from God's trust often begins with a compromising decision to tolerate a worldly plan or compromise our faith and trust in God. Satan will do everything possible to start a faith-withering process by a small cut of compromise. Satan wants to move us outside God's will because a little compromise can take us far from trusting God. Compromise is Satan's strategy, but it is not always apparent. Many have met with defeat because of compromising on some spiritual matters. Satan has devised millions of plans, policies, procedures, pills, and practices that will compromise our faith in Christ—things concerning money, healing, wrongs, work issues, relationships, school matters, or home problems. Satan always suggests a compromise whenever we want to do God's will. Pharaoh would not allow the Israelites to leave, so God brought ten successive plagues against Egypt, each building in intensity. Instead of relenting and repenting, Pharaoh became hardened and calloused. Satan wants us to be stubborn and rebellious. When God's hand of conviction is placed on something in our life, and we are unwilling to correct it, our hearts can become calloused and defiant.

Our convictions may cause discomfort when we stand amid a crowd that doesn't share our beliefs. A few days go by when we are not asked to compromise what we consider essential. We are seen as close-minded or the enemy if we decide not to compromise. We've all heard the adage that "compromise is the secret to being happy." It's common to hear compromise linked to love and compassion. On the other hand, if we're unwilling to compromise, we fear being seen as unfair, rigid, or politically incorrect. As kids, most of us were taught that compromise is an ideal method of solving a dispute and a practical framework for an agreement. Although the idea of fairness that drives compromise is well-intentioned, the reality of compromise is much less appealing. To please both parties, we end up taking a part of what each person wants and blending those parts to create a subpar agreement that both parties feel genuinely satisfied with. In a compromise, the goal is to create an arrangement where each side's wins and losses are relatively equal. In other words, each person is asked to concede something and is simultaneously awarded something they want. As a result, everyone's wins and losses are balanced, and everyone feels like they received a fair deal.

There's an old saying that "a giraffe is a horse designed by a committee." They wanted a better horse; they got something that couldn't go where horses go. In a compromise, you're attempting to take pieces of two polar solutions and somehow meld them together into one. The result is a giraffe—an arrangement that looks and feels like two disparate ideas awkwardly grafted into one. If we're focused on compromise, we're not working to build our counterparts' trust and organically influence their decisions. No matter our compromise, it will always be evaluated against their ideal solution and inevitably come up short. Even though the settlement is often attempted in the spirit of collaboration, it keeps both parties on opposite sides of the negotiation table (*your* solution versus *my* solution) rather than uniting them on the same team. In an attempt to be partisan, we often agree to compromises without genuinely thinking through the logistics of how it will be carried out. For example, two divorced parents might decide to share custody of a child, with each parent getting the child for one-half of the year. Although this agreement is (at least superficially) equal, it doesn't account for implementation. How will the child change schools? What about the holidays? Who will be responsible for what? The potential *"what about"* and *"what ifs"* are endless and unanswered. Both parties adopt a nearly impossible solution to uphold (and sabotage the agreement before it's begun) to keep things fair. Then there's the emotional toll.Even though a willingness to compromise is often likened to being flexible, the opposite is true. If you're in a position where you're considering compromise, then you have yet to explore all your options. Compromise is to make concessions or accommodations for someone who disagrees with a set of standards or roles. The Bible makes it very clear that God does not condone compromising His standards. Although there are some areas in life where compromise may be necessary, there are other areas where the center is hazardous and even deadly. James warns the believers about compromise.,

"You adulterous people, don't you know that friendship with the world is hatred toward God? Anyone who chooses to be a friend of the world becomes an enemy of God."
James 4:4

The fundamental doctrines of our faith must never be compromised. These are the very beliefs that make us uniquely Christian. So, likewise, the message of the Gospel of Jesus Christ must never be compromised. Methods of evangelism may change, but the message of the Gospel never does.

"Have I not commanded you? Be strong and courageous. Do not be afraid; do not be discouraged, for the Lord your God will be with you wherever you go."
Joshua 1:9

Compromise on some matter, issue, or decision can quickly take us outside the will of God. To compromise is to concede, give up, or forfeit some part of the standard we conduct in our life. The devil makes it easy to compromise by offering a substitute, but following any worldly plan can quickly move us away from a position of trust in God.

"Today if ye will hear his voice, Harden, not your heart, as in the provocation and the day of temptation in the wilderness."
Psalm 95:7-8

After seeing many divine miracles, Pharaoh knew of God's power, but he still became more stubborn. The soil of our heart must be ready to receive the seed of the Word so that spiritual fruit can grow—we must respond to conviction. Satan wants us to stay close to the worldly ways we had followed or retain the unscriptural attitudes we had kept—he makes it easy for us to return to them. Therefore, God commands the Israelites to travel three days from Egypt to separate them from that pagan culture. The devil tries to hinder our attending church services, and if we do attend, he wants to fill our minds with something or anything to block out the message. He wants us to forget what was heard after a service. Satan always opposes Bible reading and wants us to read late in the evening, so we fall asleep and forget everything we read. Compromise begins the process of moving away from God. Once the cutting of the branch begins, the withering process continues. The devil often tries to have someone compromise on romantic relationships with unbelievers. Still, God's Word speaks clearly on the matter.

"Do not be yoked together with unbelievers. For what do righteousness and wickedness have in common? Or what fellowship can light have with darkness?"
2 Corinthians 6:14

If we compromise on this issue, we can move away from faith in Christ of the nonbeliever's lack of faith. Unbelievers have a character that often does not want to trust God for anything. Still, a true-believing Christian has a divine nature that wants to trust God for everything. The two natures have nothing in common because the spiritual light of God's truth is directly opposite to the spiritual darkness of this world. Millions have fallen away from trusting God in faith due to close relationships with someone who has no desire to trust God in faith. We cannot be close friends with anyone uninterested in God's Truth. If we compromise on fellowship, our faith will wither. Furthermore, our eternal life can be at risk if the relationship leads to marriage.

As believers in Christ, we are responsible for standing firm on the principles of God's Truth and not compromising on faith issues. Compromise is deadly because it undermines the faith of the compromising one. The first consequence is a withering of our spiritual life—we become more tolerant of things that should be offensive. If Satan can draw *t*he children away, he will have the next generation—that is why he tries to have young people be involved with harmful things— unscriptural relationships, risk-taking, alcohol, drugs, immorality, fornication, or anything that would hinder their preparation for eternal life. The devil is determined to have the children, so he has the entertainment industry design programs that will capture their attention and interest— movies, TV shows, commercials, music, sports, and even religious films can include wrong ways, worldly attitudes, anger, violence, alternative lifestyles, or some anti-Christian message. The devil wants our children, and one way he can get them is to have their parents compromise with God's will on entertainment. The devil well knows what will influence children's minds most, so he has most households accept television. It would be complicated, if not impossible, to tell the children *not* to think like the world when we just invited the world into our home. Anyone who wants to train their children on how to meet things in a scriptural way must live God's Truth themselves because most of what is seen and heard, and read on the Internet; on computers; tablets; smartphones, social media; and many other types of communications, is opposite to the message of the Bible. Worldly attitudes can be seen in just about everything today. We must personally influence our children by living a godly life ourselves.

The devil continually tries to capture the attention and then the minds of young people, and he knows *what* will influence them. Compromise on what we view, listen to, or spend much time on, can quickly begin a faith-withering process. We must not allow Satan to have our children—as Moses refused to allow Pharaoh to have his (Exodus 10:9). Satan wants us to compromise—saying, "I'll watch sports on my tablet, smartphone, etc.," but soon include other compromising things. However, the consequence of any compromise can be a downhill slide to tolerate more and more worldly entertainment and attitudes—something that can lead us far from the will of God. Satan is stalking and (1 Peter 5:8) "seeking whom he may devour," but we are to "Resist him, steadfast in the faith;" so that "the God of all grace, who called us to His eternal glory by Christ *Jesus, after you have suffered a while, perfect, establish, strengthen, and settle you.* " When Satan tries to have us compromise—where there can be no compromise—whether it be with money, our children, fellowship, marriage, abortion, avenging wrongs, or anything else—we must say to the devil what Moses said to Pharaoh —No deals; no compromising—every child, every attitude, and every decision belongs to God, and they must glorify Him.

Notes From Reading:

Questions For The Group:

Prayer Request for Today:

Day 19

COMPARING YOURSELF WITH OTHERS?

"Not that we dare to classify or compare ourselves with some commending themselves. But when they measure themselves by one another and compare themselves with one another, they are without understanding."
— 2 Corinthians 10:12

DAILY PRAYER

Dear Lord, I have not been open to the total leadership of the Holy Spirit. I often need to remember the power available through the Holy Spirit. Please help me understand more about the Holy Spirit and how I can make Him the center of my life.

Many of us struggle by comparing ourselves to others, often thinking they are better than us. We look at magazines with photo-shopped pictures and compare ourselves to what we see. We don't see ourselves as young and toned as we were in the past; perhaps we are larger than we remember. We often look at our friends and neighbors successes and wonder why our lives haven't measured up to theirs. Comparing ourselves to others could be more helpful. But, in all honesty, it can be extremely harmful. We should consider instead seeing ourselves as God sees us! He created us and planned our existence before we were born. He made us unique with extraordinary gifts, and we have infinite value in His eyes. He loves us passionately, and He gave everything for us! Comparing ourselves to others never makes us feel better. Jesus can change our lives forever! Jesus once told the story of a man who loved to compare himself to others. He prayed like this: *"I thank You that I am not like other men.*" He loved to compare himself because he believed his religious standing made him superior. Jesus said that this man returned to his house like he came, unforgiven, unjustified. (Luke 18:11) We must stop comparing ourselves to others. It doesn't matter how many people are on our side or saying good things about us; we still feel lousy because no one wins when we make such comparisons. How often do we compare ourselves with someone less fortunate than us and consider ourselves blessed? We mostly compare ourselves with people we perceive as being, having, or doing more. We have this innate desire to know where we fit into our world. Instead of comparing ourselves to others, why not think about where we have been and where we are today?

"Why compare yourself with others?"
2 Corinthians 10:12

In our lives as Christians, we are always becoming a new creation. Who we are today is a result of the decisions we made yesterday. We are always in a state of renewal. No one can do a better job of being you than you. Jesus is the standard to measure our life, not other people. We can't find happiness in this life as long as we carry envy and jealousy. The Apostle Paul in (Philippians 3) sums this up for us:

We could be better.
We have yet to arrive.
We are a work in progress.

When comparing yourself to others, consider stopping momentarily and re-directing your thoughts. How are you trying to become a new and improved version of yourself? We focus on becoming more complete and joyful than we were last year. We must treat ourselves with respect, care, compassion, and praise. Think about the good things you have done, how you have changed, and where you are going compared to last year.

Thomas J. DeLong, a Harvard Business School professor, noted a disturbing trend among his students and colleagues. He called what he found "the comparison obsession." He wrote: "Business executives, Wall Street analysts, lawyers, doctors, and other professionals are obsessed with comparing their achievements. I have discovered that comparing has reached almost epidemic proportions." Of course, comparing ourselves to others is a bad idea, but we always do it because we are jealous.

To help His followers understand the kingdom of Heaven and the dangers of comparison, Jesus told a parable about a landowner who hired workers to tend his vineyard. He hired workers around 6:00 am. and agreed to pay them a day's wage. Then he hired workers at 9:00 am., noon, 3:00 pm., and 5:00 pm and indicated that he would pay them what *was right.*" (Matthew 20:4-5) When it was time to pay the workers, He paid them each the same wage, a denarius. The first group He hired protested, accusing the owner of being unfair. The owner reminded the grumblers that he could be controversial and scandalously generous if desired. Then he revealed the issue's root —they were "jealous" of his extravagant generosity. (Matthew 20:15)

Our homes are no longer a place to eat, sleep, and get away from to rest of the world. They have become statements about the value of our life. Sometimes they become significant, highly decorated monuments to ourselves. We all appreciate creature comforts, but how much room do we need to be comfortable? Of course, most of us also need a lot of stuff to fill our homes. A whole industry has arisen around our need to have more things than we need. Having a good job, a supportive family, a network of friends, a nice place to live, and a church home are vitally important to each of us. You have most of these. Although they are essential, they cannot be what gives us purpose and define our life. As Paul said in (Philippians 3), "*I must count them as loss* because of what Jesus has done for me. My relationship with Jesus must define my life. Everything between Jesus and me is an idol to some degree and must be dealt with." Paul says we must be willing to lose everything to have a relationship with Christ Jesus. What would you think if "T*hou shall not compare or complain*" were two of the commandments? Satan uses complaining to try and stop the work of Christ every day. He worked to derail God's plan for the Israelites and is still active today with us in his cross-hairs. So what do you think is his goal? An essential part of his plan is to get us to complain and complain, eventually giving up on Christ. God had delivered the Israelites from bondage in Egypt, yet they doubted Him when they were overwhelmed by problems. When they started their journey, many reacted with fear when the Egyptian army aggressively pursued them. But God delivered them. As they began their journey toward the Promised Land, they realized they needed food and forgot God's promises; they concluded that Moses had "*brought us out into this wilderness to kill this whole assembly with hunger.*" Many were discouraged and wished they had stayed in Egypt. They grumbled to Moses and Aaron, but Moses recognized that neither was the real target. They were complaining "*against the Lord.*" They learned each time that God kept a promise and would always meet their needs, even when things seemed impossible.

You have been in a similar situation on many accounts. No matter what your family has, more is needed. You may be upset today about a number of things: school, friends, peer pressure, or money. Although we don't usually think about it, we show our displeasure with God when we grumble. So, despite His promises, sometimes we don't trust Him. We may be frustrated, angry, bitter, or worried about many things, but we are called to be thankful for what we have. Let us take a moment and look back at how God has provided for us, and we will see that He always keeps His promises.

"My God will meet all your needs according to his glorious riches in Christ Jesus."
Philippians 4:19

Some people interpret this verse as if they had a genie in a bottle they were carrying around, just waiting to rub on it and ask for what they wanted. However, when Paul wrote these words, he was speaking from experience. Since becoming a Christian and a missionary for the Lord, he has faced almost every obstacle imaginable. He'd been imprisoned, faced persecution, and suffered at the hands of those who hated him. Yet, each time, God faithfully met his needs. God never let him down. Whether in plenty or want, hungry or well-fed, Paul had experienced God's providing hand. God promises to meet your every need, just like he did Paul. He already knows what you need and promises to ensure you receive what that is. God will be with you every step of the way, providing for you in ways that only God can. We must make sure we understand these words of Paul concerning this matter. God does not promise to give us everything we desire or pray for. Sometimes God's answer to our prayers is "*No*." Sometimes God will answer our prayers in ways we don't anticipate or like. There will be things that God will withhold from us, but He does promise to give us what we need to fulfill His purpose for our lives. How do we break this cycle of comparing ourselves with others?

Awareness. We often make these social comparisons without realizing we're doing it. It's a natural act, and as a result, it's done without consciousness. So the solution is to become conscious and bring these thoughts to the forefront of your consciousness by being on the lookout for them. If you focus on these thoughts for a few days, soon, it'll be hard not to notice.

Stop yourself. Once you realize you're making these comparisons, stop. Don't criticize yourself or feel bad; acknowledge the thought and gently change focus.

Count your blessings. A better focus is on what you have and has already been blessed with. Count what you have, not what you don't. Think about how lucky you are to have what you have and the people who care about you.

Focus on your strengths. Instead of looking at your weaknesses, ask yourself what your strengths are. Then, celebrate them and be proud of them. Don't brag, but feel good about them and work on using them to your best advantage.

Be OK with imperfection. No one is perfect, and while we all know that, we seem to feel bad when we don't reach perfection. You aren't perfect, and you never will be. Keep trying to improve and become a better version of yourself. If you look at it differently, that imperfection makes you who you are; you already are perfect.

Don't knock others down. Sometimes we try to criticize others to make ourselves feel better. However, taking someone down for your benefit is destructive, and it forms an enemy when you could be creating a friend in the end, which also hurts you. Instead, try to support others in their success, which will lead to more success on your part.

Focus on the journey. Don't focus on how you rank compared to others because life is not a competition. It's a journey; we are all trying to find something. That journey has nothing to do with how well others are doing or what they have. It has everything to do with what you want to do and where you want to go. That's all you need to worry about.

Learn to love enough. If you always want what others have, you will always need more.

It's an endless cycle, and it will never lead to happiness. No matter how many clothes you buy, no matter how many houses you own, and no matter how many fancy cars you acquire—you'll never have enough. Instead, learn to realize that what you have is already enough. You are blessed if you have shelter over your head, food on the table, clothes on your back, and people who love you. You have enough. Anything you have over and above that — and let's admit that all of us have more than that — is more than enough. Be good with that, and you'll find contentment. Jesus looks us in the eye each morning and asks, "When does it stop? When will you finish splurged for the latest " have to have it? When will you have a bigger boat? Larger house? More employees? Expensive car? When does it stop?" The Christian faith does not say it's wrong to have desires or to appreciate good things in life. Whether we are rich or poor, we must ask whether we are "rich toward God," living every moment out of gratitude for all that God has
already given us.

Notes From Reading:

Questions For The Group:

Prayer Request for Today:

Day 20

WHEN IS ENOUGH, ENOUGH?

"Do not store up treasures on earth. Store up treasures in Heaven. For where your treasure is there your heart is. No man can serve two masters. You cannot serve both God and Mammon. Do not worry about your life – what you eat – what you wear."
—Matthew 6:19

DAILY PRAYER

Lord Jesus, I want to continue on the important things to You. I want to stay steadfast in my commitments to you and those I have made, as You were my witness. Taking the wide road is much easier than the narrow path. Unfortunately, I have sometimes left the course. Please help me to be more obedient to your calling in my life.

When is enough? So most of us can picture an exasperated parent. Their children are arguing and misbehaving, and it's just time to stop things. They look at their kids and finally say, "that's it, that's enough, stop it!" When is enough enough? That phrase can also be put into question. When will I know whether or not I am doing enough? Will I ever be able to please my boss? We go home some nights with a nagging frustration that no matter how much we have done or how hard we have worked, we will never do enough. God's Word speaks to people who never seem to have quite enough to make life work, not enough time, energy, or money. Is your life such that the alarm goes off before you've had time to get your sleep, and so you wake up tired? Do you have to get up, get the children clothed and fed, and get everyone out the door? When you get to work, there's more work than you can do already waiting for you. The phone is ringing; people are stopping by; the day is filled with meetings; even lunch is a meeting. You get to the end of the day and have yet to do all the work you should have done. You either must take some home or feel guilty about not completing it. You may have to pick up children on the way home and take them to lessons, games, or sports practice. When you get home to that place that should be a place of refuge, there are chores to be done, meals to be prepared and cleaned up, lawn to be taken care of, bills to be paid, and you have more months than you have money. When is enough enough? Why is life so hectic for us? Why do some people always need more time, energy, or money? We always need a little bit more. Most of our worries are money worries. It is not by accident that Jesus, in His Sermon on the Mount, discusses worry in the section dealing with our relationship with material things. It is the most extended section because it is our biggest problem. Almost all of us have far more than we need compared to the rest of the world, and yet we are stressed out, always on the go, and our family life suffers the most.

"Your heart will always be where your riches are. No one can serve two masters. He will hate one and love the other. He will serve on and be disloyal to the other. You cannot serve God and money."
Matthew 6:21-24

The American dream, for many, has turned into a nightmare. "We buy things we don't need; with money we don't have; to impress people we don't like." When we are young, we spend our health to get wealth; when we are old, we spend our wealth to get our health back. The Ten Commandments begin with putting God first and having no other *"gods."* They end with, *"You shall not covet."* (Exodus 20) The New Testament says *"coveting"* – wanting things we do not have is "*idolatry.*" (Colossians 3:5). These are the book-ends of the Ten Commandments and are the main reason we break the eight commandments in between. Jesus used the Aramaic term "*mammon*" (money) as a personal name for the greedy person's God. (1 Timothy 4:10), "*The love of money is the source of all kinds of evil.*"

> *"You must put to death the earthly desires at work inside you; such as sexual immorality; indecency; evil passions, and greed (covetousness); because covetousness is idolatry."*
> *Colossians 3:5*

God says that wanting our way is dangerous. The church in the sixth century listed this as one of the "*Seven Deadly Sins.*" Eve had everything, but she wanted more. If you recall, it was the first sin out of Eden. A bit later, Cain killed Abel because he coveted the acceptance God gave him. It is the source, the "*root*" of almost all other sins. All six of the seven deadly sins come from it: pride (I want me to be first), greed (wanting money), lust (wanting sex), and gluttony (wanting pleasures).

> *"The love of money is the source of all kinds of evil. Some, in their eagerness to have it, have wandered away from the faith and have broken their hearts with many sorrows."*
> *1Timothy 4:6-10*

God is not in the business of ruining our fun, and He does not stay up nights thinking of ways to make you miserable. He hates sin because it hurts us. "*If you love gold, you will never be satisfied with gold. If you long for wealth, you will never be wealthy enough.*" (Ecclesiastic. 5:10) Solomon sucked up all the pleasures he could find; wealth, wisdom, work, wine, and women. And he called it "*Meaningless,*

Chasing the wind." (Ecclesiastics 1:11) Madison Avenue advertising has done a job for our families and us. It says, "Here is more. Here is something else you need." Even the right deodorant puts a smile on our faces. What we accumulate proclaims our success, and our motto is: "He who dies with the most toys wins. Once a man, twice a boy, The only difference is the price of his toys." Recently, several people worth millions and even billions of dollars broke the law and went to jail. Their crime: they wanted to get their children into colleges they weren't prepared to attend. Let's hold on to our stones because we are all a bit like them: We never have enough. Our home always needs to be nicer. Our place in the company needs to be higher. Our bank account needs to be more significant. We "get all we can. Can all we can, and sit on the can."

> *"You work and worry your way through life, and what do you have to show for it / everything you do brings you nothing but heartache and worry. Even at night, your mind cannot rest."*
> *Ecclesiastic. 2:22-23*

Marriage counselors often say that the two biggest problems in marriage are selfishness and money. At the head of the list are debit and credit cards. Gorging ourselves on more and more, our families pay a terrible price. This creates stress. The "*mad desire to acquire gone haywire*" requires extra work to make money, not for necessities but for luxuries. The tired mother and Father come home irritated already, and things like dinner, crying children, homework, teens who are playing video games, and bills make home life hectic. The more we want, the more guilt we feel, and thus the more irritable and depressed we become. We often take these feelings out on each other and our children.

Our possessions possess us. There are always things to mow, something to plant, things to paint, things to pull up, things to prop up, things to pay for, and things to ponder. When people die, one of the most challenging problems is what to do with all their "stuff." Let three cars in front of you from a side road during peak driving hours and see what happens. The man behind you makes a dirty gesture at you. We leave our $300,000 houses in our $50,000 cars, go to our six-figure jobs and explode with road rage if someone pulls out in front of us or is driving too slow. This may be why our pockets are full of pills.

A man asked Jesus to make his brother divide the family inheritance with him. Jesus sternly warned him (Luke 12:15), *"Be on guard against every kind of greed; because a person's life is not made up of what he owns."* Then he told the story of a successful man planning well for retirement (filling his barn to eat, drink and enjoy life). He wasn't planning to spend it on prostitutes or pornography; he felt he had earned the right to enjoy life before dying. Most people in America would applaud him and his portfolio, but God calls him a fool. When the last nail was driven, when the retirement income was signed for, he dropped dead. Our "god" is what we think about, work the hardest for, and love the most. And for most of us, this is material possessions. We drive our idols, wear them, and live in them. Our gods are not these things; they are *"us."* We worship ourselves, and these are our offerings to *"us."* Are you serving Him or yourself?

How much is enough? I read a column in the Rocky Mountain News that the average home built in Boulder County, Colorado, last year was 6,990 square feet. It cited that the average square footage of a home in Japan is 1,000 square feet. In Ireland, the average home has 930 square feet. In the UK, it is 815 square feet. We tend to be hard on celebrities and the rich and famous who are extravagant and live large in their behavior. Excessive living and exorbitant privilege overtake us all. If we can admit that most of us have a problem with having enough, what should we do? How about looking at people who are happy and satisfied with their life just as it is? If we spend time with people who are never satisfied and always want more and more, we'll soon find that we feel the same way. So instead, surround yourself with those who realize life is much more fulfilling and spectacular than how much they make or what they own. Hang out with happy people, regularly help others, and who knows what makes them joyful from the inside out, and start doing what they are doing.

When John D. Rockefeller, one of the wealthiest men in the world, was asked how much money was enough, he replied, "A little bit more." Even he didn't realize that you likely will only be satisfied or happy once your basic needs are covered. Let's face it; even some of the more impoverished people in your community have more than many others worldwide. Unfortunately, many spend much time focusing on losing money instead of celebrating what we have. It might be wise to start realizing that our well-being and peace of mind begin within. That is the only way we'll discover we have more than enough, just as we are right now. Here is when it is enough. Enough is enough when you have placed your faith in Jesus Christ and realize that you will live forever. Jesus is enough. You can't do enough. His enough is enough. That's the beauty of the Gospel. You are trusting in the only one who can save you. His enough is enough.

Notes From Reading:

____

____

____

____

Questions For The Group:

____

____

____

Prayer Request for Today:

____

____

____

Day 21

ARE YOU SHARING JESUS?

"Then he said to his disciples, The harvest is plentiful, but the laborers are few; therefore pray earnestly to the Lord of the harvest to send laborers into his harvest."
Matthew 9:37-38

DAILY PRAYER

Dear Jesus, I know some people need you in this world. It seems so dark sometimes with all we read in the paper and see on the news. Place me in the right place this week to step up and then give me the courage to do so.

You've heard it said many times: preach the Gospel at all times; when necessary, use words. The often-quoted statement expresses a well-meaning viewpoint for many Christians today. Some people are concerned that Christians have been too loud, demanding, and angry. They continue to say that Christians should show the Gospel by your lives, not their words. They may be correct, but something tells me it may be the opposite. We all agree that we must demonstrate the Gospel in our lives; however, it is often used as an excuse for not sharing Jesus with those around us. According to Scripture, unbelievers are not only like sheep in trouble but also like wheat that needs to be harvested. Jesus made it clear that many lost people need salvation. Many question whether the harvest is genuinely as plentiful as some believe. The harvest is indeed abundant in our homes, work, community, and family, that's for sure. Are you sharing Jesus Christ with others, or do you leave that task to others?

It is estimated that more than 4.5 billion people worldwide don't know Christ as their Savior. If not reached, these individuals will spend eternity disconnected from Jesus. Everyone does not believe this. Many are convinced that everyone will go to heaven when they die. We often want to believe that our families are just fine. However, they demonstrate no desire for the things of God, and they are many times indistinguishable from the world. We show no urgency when our children and immediate family are lost. Worse still, you may have children living in our home who don't know Jesus as their personal Savior. Many Christians condemn traditional churches because they are focused on the sweet bye-and-bye while neglecting the now-and-now. For many in our circle of influence, we are their only exposure to God. Sooner or later, people will ask us the *"important"* question, and it will be critical that we are prepared with a concrete answer.

"What good is it, my brothers, if someone says he has faith but does not have works? Can that faith save him? If a brother or sister is poorly clothed and lacking in daily food, and one of you says to them, 'Go in peace, be warmed and filled,' without giving them the things needed for the body, what good is that."
James 2:14-16

Today's media portrays Christians as close-minded and judgmental, so the last thing many Christians desire is controversy. Despite today's cultural climate toward Christians, if there has ever been a time in history when Jesus needs to be shared, it is now. When sharing Jesus with others, there is no room for *"political correctness."* The stakes are too high. This is our friends and family's eternity, and every person has the right to know God. People who don't have a well-grounded understanding of why they are here are the most vulnerable to being led astray by Satan.

One task of every Christian is undoubtedly to be a Godly example. Many do not read the Word of God for themselves and have not really experienced God. Therefore, they rely more on a Godly example than they should. This can be a dangerous path for them to follow and a stressful place for Christians. For this reason, the Apostle Paul was aware that people paid attention to his behavior and actions. He warned us to keep our distance from others who are not doing right, even if they claim to be Christians. He defines *"disorderly"* as those who are lazy and not working and those who meddle in other people's business. Association with these people may give others the impression you are just like them. Nevertheless, we must continue doing what we know to be correct. We must keep focused and not get tired, no matter what others say.

Milton Hershey, the creator of the famed Hershey Chocolate Fortune, had two favorite loves: children and chocolate. So, believing the two would go together, he opened a small chocolate factory in 1903. Hershey knew how to make good chocolate bars but didn't know much about selling them. So he figured, *"If my product is as good as I believe it is, people will tell others about it."* And that's precisely what happened. News spread simply by word of mouth. So, for several decades, Hershey never spent any money on advertising. Hershey's plan was similar to God's plan for getting His message out. God counts on millions of Christians to tell family, friends, and acquaintances that Jesus exists and is still alive. We see an example of that when He healed a demon-possessed man. The healed man begged Jesus to take him along for his ministry. Jesus said, *"Go back home and tell the folks you already know how much the Lord has done for you.*" The man did that. He told his story in a large area called the Decapolis: "*All the people were amazed.*"

"But ye, brethren, be not weary in well doing."
2 Thessalonians 3:13

Never underestimate the personal impact you can make in your everyday relationships with others. Share your story in the power of the Holy Spirit, beginning with the people you know, and stand back and see what God will do.

"For He hath put all things under His feet..."
1 Corinthians 15:27

You have heard it said, "*God will never give you more than you can handle.*" This sounds terrific and comforting during times of high stress and difficult circumstances. However, you will never find this statement in the Bible. Surprised, don't be. Things happen in our lives, and we are not equipped to handle them, and that's why we need Jesus. As Christ-followers, we are not immune from painful and sometimes impossible situations, things we can't take on alone. God has given us His support, encouragement, and strength. He uses and works through us to help each other through difficult times. The Lord also has given us the Holy Spirit, who is always with us, strengthening, empowering, comforting, encouraging, and loving us when the events and circumstances of life get too much.

"*God will never give you more than you can handle*" is a humanistic mindset, similar to "*God helps those who help themselves.*" By the way, this is also not in Scripture. Instead, it comes from the minds of humans who teach self-sufficiency instead of dependence upon God. Most of us dislike being dependent on anyone because it shows weakness.

"Boast not thyself of tomorrow; for thou knowest not what a day may bring forth."
Proverbs 27:1

We are only promised today and are told in the Bible not to boast about tomorrow as if it is guaranteed. Also, we shouldn't wait to put off tomorrow, something the Lord has called us to do today. In twenty-four hours, people will change, and today's opportunities will never be the same as they are right now. Today is the day you should do what needs to be done. Love those who need your love—minister to those the Lord has brought into your life. Life can change on a dime; unfortunately, many may not learn this until it occurs. We must be prepared when it does.

"But you will receive power when the Holy Spirit comes on you, and you will be my witnesses in Jerusalem, Judea, and Samaria, and to the ends of the earth."
Acts 1:8

A sphere is a three-dimensional, geometric object with all its points at an equal distance from a given moment. WOW--you must be impressed. In a sphere, each point on the surface is the same distance from the center. Picture yourself inside a large, hollow, glass sphere for a moment. You can reach down, up, or out from where you stand to touch every point inside the sphere. The entire area might be called your sphere of influence. Standing inside a glass sphere may sound silly, but think of it in terms of your life. You have various spheres of influence:

home, work, teams, clubs, or particular groups. You can make a difference for the cause of Christ in your sphere of influence.

When Jesus instructed His disciples in (Acts 1:8), He told them to reach out with the excellent news beginning in their immediate area and then move out into their spheres of influence. *"You shall receive power when the Holy Spirit has come upon you, and you shall be My witnesses both in Jerusalem, and in all Judea and Samaria, and even to the remotest part of the earth."* Although Jerusalem was not the disciples' home, they were told to start there. From Jerusalem, they moved on to the rest of Judea, Samaria, and finally to the remotest part of the earth.
Rather than focusing exclusively on the remotest part of the earth, we need to bloom where we are planted. We need to build relationships with those in our immediate sphere of influence to eventually widen our focus. When comfortable in a relationship, people are usually more open to an invitation to church or to talk about spiritual things. Remember, we don't build relationships for the sole purpose of getting notches on a spiritual belt. Relationships are created because people are essential to God.

Notes From Reading:

Questions For The Group:

Prayer Request for Today:

WEEK FOUR:

People Are

Always

Watching You

Day 22

ARE YOU FAKING IT?

*"Better the poor whose walk is blameless than the rich whose
ways are perverse."*
Proverbs 28:6

DAILY PRAYER

*You know me, Jesus. You understand everything about me. I have no
secrets from you, although I sometimes wish I did. Lord, peel back my
scales and help me live a life open to my family, friends, co-workers,
and especially you. Lord, help me see where I am not the man you want
me to be. Jesus, I want to live without worrying about people
discovering my secrets.*

Most of us have a public image, and we have a private one. The public
image is the one our family knows, the church, and our friends know.
However, it may not be the person who, when we are alone, others
would recognize. Flirting with the opposite sex, watching pornography,
cheating, talking wrong about people, or having a foul mouth. We desire
to live a life that is *"what you see is what you get,"* but we may not want
everyone to know our little secrets. As Christians, we are called to live a
life of transparency. When no one is looking, who you are is who you
are. We can easily fall into the trap of keeping up with the *"Jones."* Our
egos can be uncontrollable, and we sometimes enjoy a life that others
know little about. Jesus said, *"I will never leave you."* When we do
things, we hope others will never discover God is there, and He is with
us and never leaves us. He knows our every move. What we do may be
hidden from others, but not from God.

Close your eyes and imagine a world where everyone is honest, has good intentions, and looks out for one another. Now, open your eyes. The world you live in is not that place; it was never intended to be. We often act differently when placed in different situations, and hiding the truth, even being a fake, is an art that is not uncommon. Transparency can be a lost virtue. Are you tired of trying to sift through people's words and pick out what is real and what is not? Do you sometimes wonder if others know or care about what is going on in your life? A life of transparency might not be a popular idea, but transparency is where we find true freedom. When we are transparent, people can see right through us. Transparency is the ability to be seen while hiding nothing, and nothing is left in the dark.

It is challenging to live a transparent life today. People can track us on the internet, iPhone, Facebook, Twitter, and other social media outlets. A favorite option for many is a compartmentalized approach to life. However, living a compartmentalized life we believe no one else knows about can be tiring and frustrating. While we avoid transparency for many reasons, the most crippling one is the fear of being found out. We are afraid for those we love to find out exactly who we are. What would our family say if they knew our secrets? Would our church ask us to teach if they knew the real you? We are all imperfect, but our imperfections make us hide from others, and, in turn, others hide their flaws from us. Our past, sins, regrets, and shame keep us closed and disengaged from others.

"Jesus told him, "I am the way, the truth, and the life. No one comes to the Father except through me."
John 14:6

We tend to slow down if we are on the interstate running ninety miles per hour and see a State Patrolman. Why? Because we know that if they see us, they will pull us over and give us a ticket. Knowing somebody is watching us makes us think twice about doing something we shouldn't do. The psalmist tells us in Psalms 33, *"The Lord looks from heaven; He sees all the sons of men."* God sees all the good things we do and all the questionable stuff. There is no way to hide our dirty secrets from Jesus, but that doesn't stop us from trying.

In the beginning, when Adam and Eve disobeyed God, they hid in the Garden. For some reason, they imagined they wouldn't have to admit their disobedience to Him if they hid. God, of course, knew where they were and what they had done. In the days of Noah, the Bible clearly says, *"Then the Lord saw that the wickedness of man was great in the earth and that every intent of the thoughts of his heart was only evil continually."* God's vision hasn't dimmed since the days of Noah or Adam. God sees our evil deeds and knows the evil thoughts in our minds and our hearts' sinful desires. If we believe God sees all we do, shouldn't it affect how we live?

Only God knows our hearts, and only He knows who we are when others aren't present. Jesus warned, *"Do not judge, or you too will be judged."* (Matthew 7:1). From what we say and do, would we be considered a consistent Christian to those who know you? Jesus commands us to love people, not treat them as if they were below us or worthless. He said, *"By this, all men will know that you are my disciples if you love one another.*" (John 13:35). The Bible also says, "*Let your gentleness be evident to all.*" (Philippians 4:5)

God wants us to be authentic and not fake. He would prefer that we are messed-up people with honest hearts who love Him rather than perfect fakers who are convinced we don't need a Savior. Consider who Jesus chose to be his closest friends and confidants. It was an earthy, working-class group of fishermen and average guys, not the religious leaders or Jewish elite. He wanted people willing to be honest, not people who appeared to have it all together. He came for the sick, the broken, the desperate, the hungry, and the heartbroken. The people pretending to have their lives together didn't want to hear what Jesus had to say because they didn't want to be honest. They couldn't bear the thought of being just like everyone else.

The sinners loved to be around Jesus. Even though He was holy, the unholy liked to hang out with Him! But what about those who thought they were Godly and thought they were holy? The early church was known for being a group of real people. In Acts 2, Peter preached an extremely bold message, accusing the Jews of crucifying Jesus. However, something he said caused the Jews to realize he was right. They responded with the most genuine words: "*When the people heard this, they were cut to the heart and said to Peter and the other apostles, 'Brothers, what shall we do?'*" (Acts 2:37) That day, three thousand people got saved, and the early church was born. It would never have happened if the Jews had not become real. They became honest, and it changed the world! We can see the life they lived together was genuine. Every day, they continued to meet together in the temple courts. They broke bread in their homes and ate with glad and sincere hearts, praising God and enjoying all the people's favor. And the Lord added to their number daily those who were being saved. (Acts 2:46–47)

Look at the words that describe this group: glad, sincere, praising, enjoying favor with people. Imagine a group of Christians with new people drawn in by their love, sincerity, and gratitude! Isn't this the kind of faith you want to be a part of? Unfortunately, some people today feel that many Christians aren't real. The word hypocrite is their go-to word. They see Christians as saying one thing and doing another. People know when we are honest and when we're faking it. However, as we grow older, especially after we've been Christians for a long time, we tend to get a bit crusty. Instead of becoming more welcoming and concerned for others, we drift to a style of Christianity that few find attractive. Fake becomes the default setting. Real becomes something that seems too scary, vulnerable, and frightening.

Jesus was the perfect example of love and self-sacrifice. The reason is that He was more than just another religious leader. He was God in human flesh, sent from Heaven to save us from our sins by His death on the cross. In other words, take your life as a challenge—a challenge for you to discover what a faithful Christian is. No, Christians aren't perfect —and we won't be until we get to Heaven. But until then, He is with us and helps us every step of the way.

People assume that all who bear the name Christian follow the beliefs, teachings, and practices of Jesus Christ. But the Bible tells us that not everyone who accepts Christ's name is a Christian! Jesus foretold that some would claim His name but deny Him through their actions. He said they would "*call Me 'Lord, Lord,*'" but "*not do the things which I say.*" (Luke 6:46). Christ and His apostles spoke of false prophets, false apostles, and false brethren. Some people call themselves Christians. Their parents were Christians and because they go to church so are they. They like to fool themselves so they won't have to face the reality of being a fake. When we reject the Word of God and choose the world instead, we can call ourselves anything we want, but it won't save us. Only faith in Jesus Christ and obedience to Him will save us.

Those who pick and choose which parts of the Bible they like and will follow seem to be making up their religion. Being a Christian requires sacrifice; it requires us to disagree with the world and society and stand up for the Word of God, even if it gets us defriended, ostracized, or hated. It requires us to deny ourselves and be faithful and obedient.

The Bible says Satan planted weeds among the wheat, and God will leave them until Judgement Day. Then, the weeds will be burned, and the wheat will be brought safely into the barn. So, it's much easier to be a fake Christian, at least in this life, to have lots of friends, to be popular and successful without ever having to face the possibility of losing everything.

Notes From Reading:

____

____

____

____

Questions For The Group:

____

____

____

Prayer Request for Today:

____

____

____

Day 23

REAL FRIENDS ARE HARD TO FIND

"Iron sharpens iron, and one man sharpens another."
Proverbs 27:17

DAILY PRAYER

Dear Jesus, please help me find a friend that will help me become closer to You and grow my faith. Also, Lord, please help me be that type of friend to someone else. I know some guys need the same thing I do, so please put them in my life and help us grow together to become stronger Men of God.

Jackie Robinson was the first African American to play baseball in the major league. Breaking baseball's color barrier, he faced hostile crowds in every stadium he played. One afternoon while playing in his home stadium of Ebbets Field in Brooklyn, he committed an error and the fans began to boo him. He stood at second base, humiliated, while the crowd became louder. Then, without saying a word, the famous shortstop Pee Wee Reese walked over and stood beside Jackie. He put his arm around him and faced the crowd. Suddenly, the fans grew quiet. Robinson later said that arm around his shoulder and that friendship saved his career. Can you imagine being Jackie Robinson, sticking out like a sore thumb as the crowd booed you? Can you imagine the loneliness, awkwardness, and anxiety he experienced? Then along came Pee Wee Reese! Now imagine the relief, the peace, the warmth, and the comfort. In our study today, we hear this same story again. A group of awkward, anxious, and probably fearful disciples had just gotten the word their leader was about to check out, and they would be left alone. They needed a friend, and Jesus teaches that He genuinely is their friend. The real issue of this text is not whether Jesus is our friend but whether we can find real Christian friends who will hold us accountable on our journey through life.

You may have many close friends, but do you have a friend who brings out the best in you? Who can you hang out with that will make you more like Christ? A more Godly parent and spouse? We need friends who will make us better and push us to be more like Jesus. Hopefully, you will find someone who can become that Godly friend. We need friends who will tell us the truth and not judge us. Friends who will not let us take an easy path. Friends who will pray for us, and we will pray for them—friends who will keep us on course and focused on our eternal journey. I'm sure you have friends, but to whom do you discuss real problems, admit your fears, share genuine concerns, and reveal your failures? Who do you ask for help, and where can you let down your defenses? When you ask someone who their best friend is, they will often name their spouse. It is a trendy thing to do. People increasingly refer to their spouse as *"their best friend."* Men and women have considerably different definitions of friendship. By an overwhelming margin, women refer to *"trust and confidentiality."* At the same time, men described a friend as *"someone I like to hang out with"* or *"someone who takes my mind off of things."* For the most part, men's friendships revolve around activities, while women's friendships revolve around sharing. Men even use the term friend far more casually. *"Friends are people men know."* A man will describe someone as *"This is my very good friend, So-and-So"* when they had just met him five minutes before. Being a friend means allowing ourselves to be vulnerable. Some people don't want their spouse to have close friends because that takes away from their time with them. Women can say to each other, *"Do you think this makes me look too fat?"* *"If he doesn't call, I'll die."* *"Help me;*

I feel like I'm coming unglued." Men often don't show these human frailties to each other, nor do they ask one another for help. To do so beyond the adolescent years would be an admission of weakness. It isn't that men are innately insensitive or deliberately withhold affection and warmth. *"As iron sharpens iron, so one person sharpens another."* We hear this verse referenced in a sermon regarding what we should do to help each other or how a group of Christian friends should help others grow in their relationship with Christ. But we rarely look at this verse and see what it has to say. (Proverbs 27:17) is more than a verse you put on a coffee mug or place in a frame on your wall. This is the way of life that is meant to be lived by Christians.

Have you been to a fair and seen an actual blacksmith working? They were probably sweating profusely because doing the job involves a massive hot fire. They are perhaps filthy because smoke and ashes fly everywhere. There is probably a lot of noise because of all the metal's beating and hammering to form its desired shape. It is a challenging process. It is a dirty, hot, loud, and uncomfortable job that has to be done. When this process occurs in Christian men's and women's lives, it can also turn into a nasty, dirty job. That's why this process is called *"iron sharpening iron"* and not *"stuffing pillows"* or *"planting daisies."* Our feelings will usually get hurt, and things will not go smoothly when we offer ourselves up to sharpening. There will be some days when that other person reveals the deepest part of you, and you have to fall on your face before God, and it will hurt.

If you have spent time with a child lately, you probably remember how often they say, *"I can do it myself."* Their insistent declaration of independence can be amusing; however, it illustrates a serious problem with human nature—our prideful self-sufficiency. So many of us are embarrassed to admit we need help. Depending on someone else, we can be humiliated, so we forge ahead with the mantra, "*I can do it myself.*" Even when we can't. Even when we shouldn't.

God is pleased with us when we look to Him in helpless dependency and trust Him in our lives, but we are a proud bunch. We'd rather be a god than depend on one. We want to be in control. This flaw has been with us since Satan first tempted Adam and Eve. He offered them the promise of being like God if they disobeyed their creator and declared their independence from Him. God detests self-sufficient pride. When we want to be above God's rule and do things our way, we walk in pride. We need others to help us. What do you do in times of crisis? We all know the correct answer: we should take everything to God. Sometimes, however, we need the help of someone "*with some skin on.*" So, after you have given our concerns to God, who do you know that will provide you with prayers and trustworthy advice?A person that has a deep relationship with God and is willing to guide you. A friend who calms your fears by merely being part of your life. The Bible shows God's hidden hand working in mysterious and inexplicable ways. Often, this is done through other people whom God has placed in the right place at the right time. God is in the shadows, arranging things, moving things we cannot see. This may be true in your life right now. God is working, but you don't know what he is doing.

Do you remember *Alice in Wonderland*? When Alice came upon the *Cheshire Cat* sitting in the tree, she needed some help, so she stopped for some advice.

"Would you please tell me which way I should go from here?"
"Well, that depends greatly on where you want to go," said the cat.
"I don't much care where I end up going," said Alice.
"Then it doesn't matter which way you go," said the cat.

"As long as I get somewhere," Alice explained.

"Oh, you're sure to do that," said the cat, *"if you only walk long enough."*

Often, we feel like Alice and stand at a fork in the road, looking in both directions and having no idea which way to go. The cat's response offers a profound and troubling truth: if we don't know where we are going, any road will do. If we continue in a different direction, we will get somewhere. However, we shouldn't be surprised if it's not the place we want to go. Our friends can help us choose the path we need to travel.

"Know ye not that they which run in a race run all, but one receiveth the prize? So run, that ye may obtain."
1 Corinthians 9:24

Paul uses the analogy of a race to describe our lives and the need to continue until the race is won. The Lord sets the perimeters of our race —the course, the length, and how victory is obtained. Our race is not a race in the classic athletic competition sense in that we are not competing with others to see who can outdo whom. Instead, the race Paul talks about is one in which we are all involved and cheer each other on. Sometimes, we need a friend because our course has obstacles, and we'll need encouragement. Other times, we will be the encourager to a struggling friend. At the end of our race, we all want to hear Jesus say that we *"did good"* and finished strong. If we try to run this race alone, we will fail. Only God allows us to achieve victory, often through our friends. Although we each have a specific race to run, we're on a pilgrimage together.

The Lord has often used friends to encourage, strengthen, inspire, challenge, and sometimes convict himself. Their role in his life has

caused him to want to have Godly friends and be a Godly friend!
Following are some of his observations of the role of a Godly friend:

1. Godly friends sharpen each other. (Proverbs 27:17) teaches us that
"iron sharpeneth iron." A godly friend will *"sharpen"* you, and you will
"sharpen" him.

2. Godly friends assure each other through adversity. Godly friends
love each other. (Proverbs 17:17) teaches that friends love at all times—
especially in adversity. Do you have the kind of friendship that
unashamedly could declare love? The old saying is true, *"Prosperity
begets friendship; adversity reveals them."*

3. Godly friends participate with each other. (Proverbs 18:24) teaches
that friends show themselves as friendly. This is a picture of the action.
Godly friends are eager to cooperate, encourage, and help each other.

4. Godly friends rejoice for one another. A Swedish proverb states,
"Friendship doubles our joy and divides our grief." Godly friends
rejoice in the blessings of a friend. This kind of relationship is no place
for jealousy, comparison, or envy.

5. Godly friends forgive one another. Of course, friends will
eventually hurt each other—and usually unintentionally. Yet, where the
Spirit of the Lord is, there is peace. Godly friends resolve tension and
quickly forgive.

6. Godly friends do not share or harbor anger. (Proverbs 22:24)
teaches that we should avoid friendship with a furious man. Yes, there
are some people the Bible teaches us to prevent or break from. A godly
friendship will not be characterized by shared anger or bitterness.

7. Godly friends spark the truth in each other. (Proverbs 27:6) says,
"Faithful are the wounds of a friend…." Godly friends are not afraid to
lovingly and appropriately speak the truth to one another. They long to
hear the truth from each other. They recognize that everybody has "blind

spots" and rejoice that God has given them "another set of spiritual eyes" to help guide, guard, and protect.

Beyond that, godly friends rejoice in truth. They discover the truth together. They talk about truth. They encourage each other through it. Truth is the common bond of their hearts—a love for God's Word and for communicating His truth to people.

Notes From Reading:

____

____

____

____

Questions For The Group:

____

____

____

Prayer Request for Today:

____

____

____

Day 24

STAYING THE COURSE

"If you love me, you will keep my commandments."
John 14:15

DAILY PRAYER

Jesus, keeping your commandments is difficult for me. I do not keep the printed words, but I never measure up now that I understand their meaning. Something tells me you already know that. I know people are always watching what I say and what I do, so help me be faithful to what I have agreed to do. I want to keep your commandments, and I want them to help me point others to you.

We have many rules governing our lives today. The federal government has rules, our local community and our employer have regulations, and we have our own rules. We know God has His rules; however, "the world" often considers His rules only suggestions. Whether we like to admit it or not, we like having rules to know our boundaries and figure out how to live within them—following the regulations makes for a healthy society. Therefore, we desire to follow God's rules when the Holy Spirit lives within us. This urging is often so strong that we feel guilty whenever we break a Commandment and return immediately to His will. Just open the newspaper or turn on the television, and you will see that many people have lost all respect for rules. Most don't have any idea that the real source of most of our laws has been set into place by God. As a result, we see spiritual chaos, lawlessness, and wretchedness in the human heart. In nearly all present-day religious denominations, we are seeing the tendency to try to *"modernize"* and *"democratize"*

God. What if, instead of climbing Mount Sinai to receive the Ten Commandments from God, Moses had turned to the Israelites and asked: *"Hey, what do you guys think we should do?"* Considering the Hebrews' bad behavior of coveting their neighbors' wives and murdering their brothers, this would not have been a great idea. Unfortunately, some people today desire to live their lives that way. They want to make their own rules and live by them.

We live in an enlightened age where we can create rules. A group of adults between the ages of 20-36 was recently asked to offer modern alternatives to the *Ten Commandments* they believe better reflected their country's needs than the original ones. There's no *"thou shalt"* among them, nothing specifically about murder, stealing, or adultery. However, there is a version of the Golden Rule, which presumably would cover those crimes. So, will their ideas form a new moral foundation for what's to come in our world? If we are spiritual leaders for Jesus, we should know what our current generations think. This is what they came up with:

The Ten Non-Commandments.
1. Be open-minded and willing to alter your beliefs with new evidence.
2. Strive to understand what is most likely true, not believe what you wish was true.
3. The scientific method is the most reliable way of understanding the natural world.
4. Every person has the right to control their own body.
5. God is unnecessary for you to be a good person or live a whole and meaningful life.
6. Be mindful of your actions and recognize that you must be responsible.

7. Treat others as you would want them to treat you. Don't judge their perspective.
8. We have the responsibility to consider others, including future generations.
9. There is no one right way to live; we are all different.
10. Leave the world a better place than you found it.

God expects absolute obedience from us. 1 John 3:4 identifies that sin is lawlessness, and we commit a sin when we break any of these commands. Let us remember that Jesus, in his Sermon on the Mount, put a much sharper edge on the commandments: *to be angry without cause was to be guilty of murder; to lust after a woman was to commit adultery.* The Bible also tells us that we are guilty of breaking them all when we break one commandment. Many believe that although they had broken one, two, or three of these Commandments, they were not guilty of breaking the Big ones. In Jesus' Sermon on the Mount, Jesus tells us these words;

"Think not that I am come to destroy the law or the prophets: I am not to destroy, but to fulfill. For verily, I say unto you, Till heaven and earth pass, one jot or one tittle shall in no wise pass from the law, till all be fulfilled. Whosoever, therefore, shall break one of these least commandments and teach men so, he shall be called the least in the kingdom of Heaven: but whosoever shall do and teach them, the same shall be called great in the kingdom of Heaven."
Matthew 5:17-19

Commandments are commands, not suggestions, written on the hearts and revealed in Christians' walk. Ted Koppel, ABC's original *Nightline* host for decades, was brought in to address the graduating class at Duke University. In his speech, he was brilliant:

In place of truth, we have discovered facts; for moral absolutes, we have substituted moral ambiguity. We now communicate with everyone and say absolutely nothing. And then he said, What Moses brought down from Mount Sinai were not 'The Ten Suggestions. They are commandments. The sheer brilliance of the Ten Commandments is that they codify acceptable human behavior in a handful of words, not just for then or now, but for all time.

Good job Ted, you nailed it.

We are not flawless people. We are not masters of our destiny, and our abilities are not limitless. Nevertheless, God knows we are dust. He is filled with compassion because of His frank and accurate assessment of our human condition. God knows us, and He knows that we fail. He will not condone rebellion or excuse sinful behavior. Still, He has a genuine understanding and is quick to forgive. Our world is filled with scam artists and people bending the truth for their benefit. We should carefully examine their claims, especially when they want access to our money. Similarly, the devil continues selling beliefs and behavior that deny or twist the Gospel's message. Followers of Christ must be aware of distorted beliefs and deceptive doctrines. We must be equipped by God's Word and stay the course of true faith.

I remember reading about an incident on the Italian Riviera years ago. A young man was driving his sports car along the ocean. It was a beautiful and scenic route, but the road seemed different. All along the way were warning signs. Yet, to the young man, the road seemed perfectly acceptable. Disaster awaited him. A landslide had recently created a tragedy waiting to happen. No one should have been on that road, but he continued quickly. He ignored all the warning signs. He went straight over the cliff. Sometimes, we are still determining where a path will lead. Occasionally, we know where it leads but choose to follow it.

"Enter through the narrow gate. Wide is the gate, and broad is the road that leads to destruction, and many enter through it. But small is the gate and narrow the road that leads to life, and only a few find it."
Matthew 7:13-14

Jesus said there is a path that leads to life. Unfortunately, there is also a path that leads to destruction (Matthew 7:13–14). Warning signs are not put up as a threat but out of love. The signs on the Italian Riviera were erected to keep people safe. The words of Jesus, the New Testament, and the Bible are designed to keep us on the path that leads to life. The busyness of life can quickly overtake our spiritual disciplines. But Jesus places us in situations in which we will have the opportunity to verbalize our commitment. Jesus pointed out Peter's weakness in understanding the life-and-death nature of the decisions before him. Peter failed, but Jesus restored him and changed his life. (John 21:15-19) "*Stay the course*" is an old nautical navigation term, meaning "*to continue in the proper direction.*" It was later used by Winston Churchill, Ronald Reagan, and George Bush as an appeal not to give up or turn back. Often, we use the term to encourage others to continue in the direction in which they started. Unfortunately, many fads and distractions threaten to sidetrack us from our calling today, so it is a good idea to consider what "*staying the course*" looks like as we venture into an unpredictable future.

Staying the course is dependent on adjusting our course. An aversion to course correction is a recipe for navigational failure. But how are these adjustments made? Our navigational course is between our present location and our intended destination. Navigational adjustments are made when we realign yourself with our desired destination. Looking back at where you've come from could be more helpful in navigation. Setting a course for your chosen destination is everything. If our destination is wrong, our course is hopeless and staying, and the course will be fruitless. As one humorist said, "*Staying the course does not mean banging your head against the wall until you die.*" Life would be easy if you could discover an easy formula for success, keep repeating the past, and be assured of future success. But life is unpredictable and in a constant state of change. What worked last year may not work next year. What works for someone else may work better for you. So, staying the course does not mean repeating the past and just doing what you've always done the way you've always done it. So, as we set our courses for the future, what is our desired destination? What should our approach be?

"One thing I do: forgetting those things which are behind and reaching forward to those things which are ahead, I press toward the goal for the prize of the upward call of God in Christ Jesus."
Philippians 3:13-14

Paul wasn't interested in repeating the past. Instead, he forgot the past so that he could focus on Jesus. In pursuit of Jesus, Paul did a lot of great things. He planted churches, but that wasn't his goal. He was an influential evangelist, but that was not his focus. He had strong ideas about government and politics, but that didn't drive him. He knew the past, but changing the future was what he majored in. He wrote fourteen books of the Bible, but even the Bible wasn't his compass. His singular goal was simply Jesus. We must follow Paul's lead well and ensure that our purpose, prize, and desired destination are merely Jesus.

It is so easy to be drawn away by the enticement of the latest fads and by whatever new gimmick promises us a shortcut to success. We can sometimes react against that temptation by retreating and withdrawing to a more secure past that may not carry us forward to God's plans. Let's stay the course. Let's set our compass on Jesus and be willing to adjust our course to align with Him.

Notes From Reading:

____

____

____

____

Questions For The Group:

____

____

____

Prayer Request for Today:

____

____

____

Day 25

USING YOUR TIME WISELY

*"As long as it is the day, we must do the works of him who sent me.
Night is coming when no one can work."*
John 9:4

PRAYER FOR TODAY

God, I love you. I am so busy. I feel pulled in every direction. Please help me focus on the one thing you call me to do—Bring glory to You. As I go through my day, help me realize everything I do that brings glory to You is my purpose. Show me, Lord, how to get glory to you in everything I do. I love you, Jesus.

The older we get, the more we realize how valuable our time is. When you are 20, 60 seems old. When you are 50, 60 is young, and 80 is older, but not old.

"Why, you do not even know what will happen tomorrow. What is your life like? You are a mist that appears for a little while and then vanishes."
James 4:14

You have heard the slogan, *"Time is money,"* but money can be redeemed when lost. Unfortunately, the same cannot be said for time. Do you often ask yourself, *"Where does all my time go?"* If this question troubles your heart every night when you go to bed, you know there's something drastically wrong with what you are doing with your life, and you are not alone. Like you, many others feel the pinch when they think of where their time is going. Let's take, for example, the life of an average, hard-working guy. He lives in Houston. He has a loving wife and a four-year-old son. He is a small business owner. Though he was proud of himself for starting his dream venture, he quickly grew unhappy with his business because he was always busy. This also impacted his relationship with his wife and son, who complained about him not being around. Every day, he had too much on his platter. It was the same old things, with emails, juggling bank accounts, attending meetings, etc. He worked hard to meet both ends – his work and his family. But the harder he tried, the more he failed. He dreamed of taking his business international, but his hopes were crushed when he started to notice that his clients and his profits began to fall because of the erratic schedules he had to work with as a small business owner and also because he had other responsibilities as a family man. His world started to fall apart. One evening, he returned to find his wife frustrated. She threw a fit because he had forgotten their anniversary. *"How could you forget our anniversary?"* she yelled. He slowly realized that he desperately needed a quick solution to balance his work and life. Otherwise, he risked losing them both. To make matters worse, he didn't find time to play with his son either. Suddenly, twenty-four hours in the day were not enough for him. He wished he had just one more hour in the day to sort his life out and get his business back in order. That's when reality struck him. He had let his business and personal life slip out of control because he believed he could handle everything alone. He slapped his head in embarrassment and asked himself, *"Where did all my time go?"*

If this story rings a bell or feels familiar, ask yourself one more question, *"How are you spending your time?"* We should be serious about our time as we don't have much of it. We never know how long we have. The Bible says, *"Prepare to meet your God."* (Amos 4:12). Be ready at all times.

"Be ready, for the Son of Man is coming at an hour you do not expect."
Matthew 24:44

The big question for us today is, *"Are we using our time in a way that is pleasing to Jesus?"* Ultimately, that's all that matters. We don't know how many more years we have and we know that tomorrow is not guaranteed. We may not live to see our next birthday, but the significant issue we all face is whether we use our minutes, hours, and days to glorify God or squander His precious gift. Time is precious because it is short. The scarcity of anything causes us to set a higher value on it, especially if it's something we can't do without. It's the principle of Supply and Demand. Prices go up if there is a great demand and a limited supply. James 4:14 says, *"Yet you do not know what your life will be like tomorrow. You are just a vapor that appears for a little while and then vanishes away."* Time is but a blip compared to eternity. Thus, we should consider it very precious. *"Time is so short, and the work we must do in it is so great that we have none to spare."*

We know time is short. Whether we have several years, a year, a month, a week, or just today— we don't know. If a man were to go on a journey through the desert on a camel and only had a certain amount of water that he could take on the trip, and he didn't know how long it would take for him to cross the desert, how precious would every drop of that water become because he doesn't know whether the water will last until he finds more. Even so, how much more should we value our time since we don't know how much of it we have left?

Time is precious because you can't get it back once it is gone. There are many things that, if we lose, we can still get back. If we lose our house or job, we can buy another home or get another job. If we were to become bankrupt and lose everything, there would always be a chance to regain all that we had lost through diligence and hard work. But when time is gone, it is gone forever. We don't usually consider time to be precious. Where would we be if we were as wasteful with our money as we are with our time? What would you think of someone who made it a habit when he was paid to light a match and burn his paycheck? Something is wrong with this guy! He's insane. Well, sometimes we do the same thing with our time. Will we all have to account for our use of time?

"You are not your own. You have been bought with a price; therefore, glorify God in your body."
1 Corinthians 6:19-20

If we are not our own, our lives are not our own, our money is not our own, and our time is not our own. Scripture teaches that Christ has bought us at the price of His precious blood. Therefore, we are no longer slaves of sin and Satan but servants of Jesus Christ. If that is true, we have no right to treat our talents, money, possessions, or time as our own. All of these things belong to Jesus.

"But I tell you that they shall give an accounting for every careless word that people speak in the day of judgment. For by your words, you will be justified, and by your words, you will be condemned."
Matthew 12:36-37

You have heard the parable of a wealthy nobleman who went to a distant country to receive a kingdom for himself and then returned. He called ten of his slaves and gave them about $20,000 to do business until he returned. Some of his slaves were diligent in using the money to advance the interests of their masters. However, one slave did nothing with the money except put it in a handkerchief for safekeeping. That parable is about us. We are the slaves, and Jesus is the nobleman who went on the journey and will one day return. While He is away, he wants us to diligently use what He has given us to advance His interests. One of the most important things He has given us is our time! Notice that in the parable, when the Master returned, He ordered that the workers be called to him so that he might know what business they had done. As a result, they were called to account. We need to use our time wisely now because one day, we will give Him an account of what we have done with it!

So the question today is, *"How will you use the remaining time God has given you?"* One of the idols we don't even think about is entertainment. We often feel this need to be entertained and amused all the time. We spend lots of money and time ensuring we are always delighted. Should we invest most of our free time day after day, week after week, and month after month primarily on meaningless amusements and entertainment? Now is an excellent time to change that pattern. Changing patterns can be very difficult because, after a while, we do certain behaviors without thinking. Today, let us break some old habits and establish some new ones.Do you procrastinate? Procrastination is *"replacing high-priority actions with tasks of lower priority or doing something from which one derives enjoyment, and thus putting off important tasks later."* Procrastination is the downfall of many of us. Putting things off will relieve our stress and solve our problems. However, we know that it only makes things worse. Essential tasks don't get done; stress is higher, not lower, and we need to remember what we did with the time we used instead of doing what needed to be done. If we want to use our time wisely, we must deal with procrastination. What is your biggest time waster? According to various polls done on the internet, these are among the top ones:

1. TV
2. Surfing the internet
3. Facebook
4. Emails
5. Cell Phones
6. Texting

We aim to spend our time loving God and loving people. If we do those things to love God and people, it's not wasted time. If you are doing them to entertain yourself so that you won't be bored, they probably are. If you are emailing or Facebooking to encouraging someone in the Lord, that is a good use of time. But if you are spending hours just checking on everyone's status, that would qualify as wasted time. *You may think, "That's all well and good, but I can't think of anything with any eternal significance for which I could use my time!"* OK, why not spend some time thinking this out for yourself? What about:

1. You are cultivating your relationship with the Lord (Scripture reading, memorizing, meditation, prayer, fasting, singing). This is the most important thing you can do with your time, bar none! Nothing is more important than spending time with God and hearing from Him. We discuss spending a reasonable amount of time with Jesus, soaking up His Word, and praying about your reading.
2. Meeting with another believer for mutual discipleship and encouragement. If you are a new believer, find a more mature believer to meet with to help you grow. At the same time, find

someone younger in the Lord than you and pour your life into
them.

3. Email or send a card or note to someone struggling with a hard
    time or sin and encourage them with Scripture.
4. Meet with another believer or 2 for prayer once a week.
5. Volunteer to help in a Christian ministry, such as a jail or prison
    ministry, crisis pregnancy center, homeless shelter, or food
    distribution for the poor.
6. Make up bags of non-perishable food items, socks, bibles, and
    tracts and give them to the homeless and poor when driving
    around town.
7. Identify a need in the church and seek to meet that need.
8. Prepare a meal for someone who is sick or just got out of the
    hospital.

You may think, *"I don't have time for all that stuff!"* We do have the
time. You may not want to use your time this way, but you have the
time. We invest our time in those things we want to do. We all have
time; that's not the issue. The real problem is how we use the time we
have. We want to be entertained, have fun, and indulge our flesh, so we
often use our time to do those things. As long as we breathe in our lungs
and our hearts are still beating, we can use our time for Jesus. So, let's
commit today to using our time for the glory of God. Some may think,
*"I have been wasting my time all my life! I have spent my time the way I
wanted to rather than how God wanted me to. I have been absorbed in
entertaining and amusing myself. In contrast, I have neglected using my
time to love God and people."* If that is true, go to God today, repent,
and receive forgiveness through the Gospel. Christ died for all our sins,
including squandering His precious gift of time. Thank God that our
standing with Him is not dependent on our perfect performance. It is
based on His grace.

Notes From Reading:

Questions For The Group:

Prayer Request for Today:

Day 26

DON'T GIVE UP

"I press on toward the goal for the prize of the upward call of God in Christ Jesus."
Philippians3:14

DAILY PRAYER

Lord Jesus, I want to continue on the essential things to You. I want to stay steadfast in my commitments to you and those I have made, as You were my witness. Taking the wide road is much easier than the narrow path. I have sometimes left the course. Please help me to be more obedient to your calling in my life.

How strong are you when it comes to persevering through troubles? We have heard all our lives *don't quit*, stay with it no matter what. However, today it seems people quit more often today than ever before. God wants us to be strong finishers. To finish strong, we can't stop along the way. One of today's new slogans is, *"If it doesn't feel right, don't do it."* People leave their jobs, walking away from marriages, children, families, and friends at an alarming rate. Jesus tells us to stick with Him to get the prize we all desire—eternity with Him. Your children have probably tried it all. You have driven them to sports practices, music teachers, unending dance recitals, and to try out after trying out. You have ensured they have had an opportunity to participate in the school talent show, student government, small groups, and church camp. Ultimately, they may have yet to commit to any of these activities, but you sure did. Sometimes, quitting seems necessary, even quitting the right things. Our children quit their teams, music lessons, art classes, and church youth programs. Sometimes, they go because they are bored, sometimes because they don't like the coach, and sometimes just because they would rather play on their phones at home.

"And let us not grow weary of doing good, for in the due season, we will reap if we do not give up."
Galatians 6:9

We have so many ways to enrich our family's lives that sometimes we quit an activity due to frustration or boredom. We often regret things that we stopped, not because we enjoyed them, but because if we had stuck it out and reached any competency, we might have found our niche. Learning to endure something even when it becomes dull or unpleasant seems a lesson truly worth remembering. Have you ever felt like you were in a hopeless situation, and the only thing you could do was quit and never look back? There was a point in his life when Paul found himself in serious trouble, so much trouble that it placed his and others' lives around him in mortal danger. We are told they were on a small ship caught up amid a tremendous storm. This was not Paul's only trouble; he had already been arrested and was going to Rome to stand trial. He was on this ship caught during a turbulent and life-threatening storm, which was more trouble! Isn't that just like life; sometimes, before we can put one problem to rest, we find ourselves assaulted by another. We are bombarded with another before we can get one thing straightened out. No one can better testify to that fact than Job. As you may recall, he faced a series of problems that came one after another.

It would have been Job if anyone in the Bible had a good reason to lose hope. He lost everything. Satan took it all from him. He lost his children, his servants, his animals, his crops, and all his possessions. If that wasn't enough, he was afflicted with painful sores from the soles of his feet to the top of his head. Job was an outstanding man of God, and Satan knew that. So, if anyone knew what it was like to feel total despair, it was Job. He was so down that he even thought his life would be better if he died. Job had lost hope, and he was ready to give up.

"Oh, that I might have my request, that God would grant what I hope for, that God would be willing to crush me, to let loose his hand and cut off my life! Then I would still have this consolation— my joy in unrelenting pain— that I had not denied the words of the Holy One."
Job 6:8-13

Job's story, how he felt, and how he reacted relate to us today because the temptation to throw in the towel and give up is universal. Every day, people go through tough situations. Every day, people decide whether to throw in the towel and give up or make a stand and pursue victory. Married couples give up on each other. Parents give up on their children. Employees give up on their jobs. The common denominator when a person is ready to throw in the towel is the loss of hope.

There is a temptation to throw in the towel when the enemy attacks, and even if we don't throw in the towel, a quiet depression often creeps into our lives. But Job didn't quit, nor should we leave because we have the same God he had to get us through our problems. Years ago, a woman from Tennessee survived a frightening experience when visiting Palm Beach, Florida. While enjoying a beautiful day at the beach, the tide suddenly carried her out to sea. Being fit, she could hold on to a buoy as she floated by. The Coast Guard found her twenty hours later, still clinging to that buoy. She received treatment for hypothermia but otherwise was in good condition. Can you imagine clinging to a buoy all night long, not knowing whether anyone would ever come to rescue you or not? She must have been tired and cold, but she still held onto the buoy despite getting colder by the minute and waves pounding her the entire time.

One of my favorite stories about Mother Teresa occurred shortly before her death in September, 1997. She planned a visit to the office of super-lawyer Edward Bennett Williams. She aimed to enlist Williams' assistance in building a hospice clinic for AIDS patients. Williams had learned the purpose of her visit beforehand. He confided to his friend, Paul Dietrich, that AIDS was not his favorite charity. He worked on a polite refusal, which he practiced before Mother Teresa's arrival. When she arrived, she made her proposal. Williams said nicely and firmly that he was sorry but could not help. Mother Teresa said, "Let us pray," and bowed. Williams rolled his eyes, but he turned his head. Mother Teresa prayed. After her prayer, Mother Teresa once again asked Williams for money to build the AIDS hospice center. She made the same appeal that she had made before her prayer. Williams again politely but firmly told her he was sorry but couldn't help. Mother Teresa said, "Let us pray." Williams rolled his eyes again, but what was he going to do? He bowed his head again as Mother Teresa prayed. He saw the handwriting on the wall. Mother Teresa had him trapped in his own office. Finally, when she ended her prayer, Williams said, "All right! All right!" and pledged his support to her cause.

Jesus tells a story like this when a widow came to a judge, asking for justice. This was a wicked judge who cared nothing about God or anyone else. His only concern was his welfare. The rich and powerful could count on a full hearing in his court, but all else need not apply. The widow was the opposite of rich and powerful. When her husband died, she lost her income and her property. She had nothing, and, as far as everyone was concerned, she was nothing. She could not expect help from the wicked judge, but she tried anyway. She demanded justice, day after day, and would not take "*no*" for an answer. Finally, the corrupt judge said: "*Though I neither fear God nor respect man, yet because this widow bothers me, I will defend her, or else she will wear me out by her continual coming.*" In other words, "*I'll do whatever it takes to get this woman off my back.*" Jesus said, "*Won't God avenge his chosen ones, who are crying out to him day and night?*" In other words, "*If a wicked judge will grant justice to those who ask, won't our loving Father do the same?*"

> *"For I know the plans I have for you, declares the Lord, plans for welfare and not for evil, to give you a future and a hope."*
> *Jeremiah 29:11*

Have you ever prayed and prayed for an answer? Have you ever gone through tough times that seemed never to end? Have you ever felt that you were at the end of your rope? Have you ever wondered if God truly cares? God is there! God cares! God answers prayer! God will vindicate the person who continues to pray through the tough times, who continues to hope, and who clings to faith. God does not answer every prayer we ask the way we desire nor does Hw answer prayers according to our timetable. Christians suffer just like everyone else. Sometimes, the good guys appear to be losing, and sometimes, the bad guys seem to win.

The story is told of a not-so-successful salesman who asked an extremely successful salesman about the secret of his success. The successful salesman said, "*There's no great secret. You have to keep jumping at every opportunity that comes along.*" The first salesman said,

"*But how do you know when an opportunity is coming?*" The successful salesman responded, "*You don't! You have to keep jumping!*"

We cannot predict the moment that God will bless us or vindicate us, but as we keep praying, we keep the channel of blessings open. This parable of the widow and the wicked judge is Jesus' promise that if we keep the channel open and persist, God will use it to bless us—not always as we want—not always as we ask—but better than we could ever imagine.

> *"Have I not commanded you? Be strong and courageous. Do not be frightened and dismayed, for the Lord your God is with you wherever you go."*
> *Joshua 1:9*

Notes From Reading:

____

____

____

____

Questions For The Group:

____

____

____

Prayer Request for Today:

____

____

____

Day 27

Being Different

" Do not conform to the pattern of this world, but be transformed by renewing your mind. Then you can test and approve God's will—his good, pleasing, and perfect will."
Romans 12:2

PRAYER FOR TODAY

God, I love you. I want to be liked, but I want to be true to you. Being different is hard. Going with the flow is more comfortable. Please allow me to stand up for you and my beliefs when questioned. Let my life tell your story as best I can. I love you, Jesus.

As Christians, aren't we are supposed to be different? We know from Scripture the answer to this question. *"Let your light shine before men, that they may see your good deeds and praise your Father in heaven."* (Matthew 5:16)

"You are a chosen people, a royal priesthood, a holy nation, a people belonging to God, that you may declare the praises of him who called you out of darkness into his wonderful light."
1 Peter 2:9

Christians and "the world" often seem to share the same obscene language, hopelessness in our conversations, and cynical attitudes about life. We are seemingly the same. We read the same books. Our dress is the same. Our drinks are the same. Our movies and television-watching habits do not deviate from those who do not share our Christian faith.

We look a whole lot like the culture in which we live. We even separate our "*spirituality,*" just like our culture, not mixing it with the rest of our lives. If Christianity and our culture are the same, why bother with being a Christian? Are we to blend in? What about the Scripture passage that tells us to "*be holy, for I am holy*" in (1 Peter 2:16)? "*Holy*" means to be "*set apart.*" Different. Are there Christians you don't want to act like?

We don't see God in their judgmental attitudes and their "*forced by condemnation and ridicule*" manipulation of people. Should there be a noticeable difference between Christians and "*the world?*" Should Christians be so "*set apart*" from the rest of "*the world*" that it renders Christians unable to witness to them? Indeed, we need not compromise or become "*soft*" toward the things identified by God as sins. But, as those "*set apart*" as "*lights shining before others,*" can we lead out of the darkness if we don't look beyond ourselves?

Christians come in all shapes and sizes. We pursue the same diversity of occupations and interests as everyone else. We have similar political and economic opinions. Most of us spend our working lives balancing budgets, living in chaos, paying off mortgages, raising kids (or electing not to have them), and generally coping from the cradle to the grave. But there is something different about most Christians once you peel away the first layer of the onion. We are not the same inside. We think differently, and our lives are guided by principles that only sometimes make sense. We handle problems differently. Our conversations are not the same as those of our non-Christian friends. Sometimes, we are harassed because we are different. At other times, we are respected for our steadfastness. People sometimes regard us as either weird and eccentric or "normal," depending on their worldviews and experiences.

What makes us different? Why do we need to stand out in a post-modern world? Why should we think differently? Why should our life priorities and activities often differ from those of our neighbors? As Christians, how can we hang out with our friends and neighbors and demonstrate that we are familiar but different for excellent reasons to enrich their lives and attract them to Christ?

As Christians, we should have a different view of the meaning of life. The Bible teaches God has made us in his image for a relationship. We believe God is involved in the world and wants to guide our lives and bless us. When we become Christians, we are "born again" and start life over as a member of a new creation, in a sense, a new race. We have a unique DNA. The Bible says they have become partakers of God's nature (2 Peter 1:4). The life of God has been implanted in us (like a computer chip), and our spirits have been made alive with God's life.

We also have a different view of relationships. Instead of being in relationships with others for *"what's in it for me,"* we believe our primary relationship is with God. Christians who implement God's word are given the strength to live in marriage, family, work, and community in terms of higher relationship principles than the world prescribes. Christians believe they are children of God, adopted sons and daughters, and other Christians are our extended spiritual family. We draw on divine strength to forgive, reach out to unlovely and unloving people, and work with more highly tuned interpersonal skills. Non-Christians cannot explain this adequately because they must identify the active ingredient.

The fact that Christians are *"different"* can be dangerous. In some countries, governments do not know what to do with people in the community whose first allegiance is not to the nation-state. So they are arrested, tortured, pressured to change, buckle under, and subscribe to parties and image-makers policies. Christians find it impossible to do this if the party or state contradicts Biblical teaching.

"We ought to obey God rather than men."
Acts 5:29

We know we cannot serve two masters, but we often try. We can be good patriots and loyal citizens, obey the law, pay taxes, and work for social stability. Still, we must be careful not to sell ourselves to a lower bidder. In many cases, Christians will always stand out to the displeasure of those in authority. Jesus said, *"If any man loves me, let him follow me so that where I am, there will my servant be also."* (John 12:26). If we act differently, this is because we are undergoing a process the Bible calls *"sanctification."* This word means *"separated."* When we follow Christ, we are separated. We no longer belong to ourselves. We belong to God. The non-Christian world stresses uniformity. Christians emphasize conformity to Christ. (Romans 12:2) The world says, *"Be like us."* The Bible says, *"Do not let the world squeeze you into its mold."*

The non-Christian world says, *"Live it up; you have only one life."* Our life is based on being *"crucified with Christ"* (Galatians 2:20; Colossians 2:20) and being *"dead"* to the world so that we can live for Christ. (Romans 6:1-7) That makes every Christian different but for the right reasons. We are not called to be rebels or mavericks but to be surrendered to Christ and the direction of the Holy Spirit. We will have different priorities, occasionally conflicting with everybody else's expectations. Still, we can also be powerful magnets attracting others to the Christ who lives within us.The thing that makes us different is what transforms us. It is a new way of thinking with new goals, desires, drives, appetites, ambitions, and key satisfaction measures. The Holy Spirit is our Teacher and mentor. (John 14:25-26; 16:13-15) Other Christians are our community of supporters who encourage us. We are different from the rest of the world for the same reasons Jesus was different. At times, we feel inadequate, but we have what many people are looking for, and they recognize it when they see it.

So what makes us different? God does. When we allow God to carry out his work in our lives, we undergo a process of metamorphosis, of radical change. We no longer think, act, or speak the same way. *"The old has gone, the new has come."* (2 Corinthians 5:17). A supernatural transformation has occurred. That is why we are different. That is why every person needs a personal encounter with Jesus; he will change your life.

Notes From Reading:

Questions For The Group:

Prayer Request for Today:

Day 28

BEYOND REPROACH?

"An overseer, as God's steward, must be above reproach. He must not be arrogant, quick-tempered, a drunkard, violent, or greedy for gain."

Titus 1:7

DAILY PRAYER

God, I love you. I am so busy. I feel pulled in every direction. Please help me focus on the one thing you call me to do—bring glory to You. As I go through my day, help me realize that everything I do that brings glory to You is my purpose. Please show me how to bring glory to you in everything I do. I love you, Jesus.

U.S. Marine Corps recruiters are "*looking for a few good men (women).*" Unfortunately, only some qualify for this highly disciplined and well-respected elite group of soldiers who have often led the way in many battles. Recruits must survive a series of grueling physical and mental tests before they become full-fledged Marines. Merely signing up is just the first step. Jesus is also looking for a few good men and women to model the Godly attitudes and actions that should be the mark of all mature Christians. It takes special people with unique characteristics to care for and nurture His people. The qualifications are extensive and essential because the job has eternal consequences.

Scripture describe the characteristics needed to serve as a pastor and elder. And although you might not be called to either position, you are indeed called to live your life set aside for Christ. The character qualifications of elders can be considered God's calling on all

Christians. While elders are meant to exemplify these traits, we must display them as Christians. Let's consider whether we exhibit these traits and learn how to pray to have them more significantly. While there are many qualifications to explore, one that seems to have special meaning today is the qualification of being *"above reproach."*

"Therefore an overseer must be above reproach"
1 Timothy 3:2

Whatever it means to be above reproach, it is not only for elders or church leaders. Colossians 3 teaches that every Christian's great hope and comfort is that God will one day *"present you holy and blameless and above reproach before him."* (Colossians 1:22) Every Christian is to be and to live above reproach. What does it mean to be above reproach? *"Above reproach"* indicates a kind of innocence in the eyes of the law. It means no one can legitimately rebuke you or make any charges against you that will stick. They may accuse you, but your conduct will eventually acquit you by proving you blameless ("blameless" is a far more common translation than "above reproach"). Your life will be so consistent that your reputation is credible, you are an example worth following, and you do not make the Gospel look fake by teaching one thing while doing another. Naturally, we must know the rules before which we must be found blameless and the standard we must uphold. In his book *Biblical Eldership*, Alexander Strauch explains that *"What is meant by "above reproach is defined by the character qualities that follow the term."* Thus, being *"above reproach"* is expressed through those other qualities in 1 Timothy 3:2, Titus 1, and 1 Peter 5. Being above reproach in your marriage means you are *"the husband of one wife."* Being above reproach in your thought life means you are *"sober-minded."* Being above reproach in your actions means you are *"self-controlled."* What we see is that this is a kind of summary attribute and that the blameless Christian is the one who upholds God's revealed will. Of course, being above reproach does not mean being perfect. But it does mean that when we sin, we confess and turn from it because our standard is perfection. (Matthew 5:48)

The primary means through which we gain this characteristic is taking advantage of God's means of grace:
- reading the Bible and deliberately applying it
- praying privately and with our family
- faithfully attending your church's worship services
- participating in the sacraments

These are the very means through which God extends his sanctifying grace, and we cannot expect to be or remain above reproach if we neglect them. As we examine the more specific character qualifications, we will be able to evaluate our life more thoroughly. There are many leadership lessons we can learn from Scripture. But, since Paul wrote 13 books, or about 28 percent of the New Testament, we could quickly fill books with his lessons. God can use anyone to carry out His mission. Since you have dedicated your life for these forty days to become closer to Christ, you will find some things for you to consider to be a leader along your spiritual journey with Jesus. Throughout the New Testament, we see that Paul was bold in his proclamation of the Gospel.

"For I am not ashamed of the gospel, for it is the power of God for salvation to everyone who believes, to the Jew first and also to the Greek."
Romans 1:16

As a leader, he did not worry about pleasing people or being liked. We can never make everyone happy. And wanting to do so is a setup for disappointment or failure. We should never be surprised when we face opposition. In (John 15:18), Jesus told his followers, *"If the world hates you, know that it had hated me before it hated you."*

Are you publicly committed to Jesus Christ? Anyone desiring to be a leader for Christ should be able to demonstrate their commitment to Jesus by their desire and faithfulness to consistent attendance at church. We are called to support every aspect of the ministry of Christ. For instance, do you participate in church events, activities, Bible studies, and discipleship opportunities? If following Christ is essential to you, your life will focus on the importance of being a champion for the church.

"In all things, I have shown you that by working hard in this way, we must help the weak and remember the words of the Lord Jesus, how he said, 'It is more blessed to give than to receive."
Acts 20:35

Do you demonstrate Godly character and values in every area of your life? Spiritual leaders must be Godly people who set the example for desired behaviors. You must demonstrate biblical principles of communicating, decision-making, and ethical behaviors in every area of your life. Believers must have high integrity and adhere to honesty and moral and ethical principles.

"If anyone aspires to the office of overseer, he desires a noble task. Therefore, an the overseer must be above reproach, the husband of one wife, sober-minded, self-controlled, respectable, hospitable, able to teach, not a drunkard, not violent but gentle, not quarrelsome, not a lover of money. He must manage his own household well, with all dignity, keeping his children submissive, for if someone does not know how to manage his household, how will he care for God's church?"
1 Timothy 3:1-13

Notes From Reading:

Questions For The Group:

Prayer Request for Today:

WEEK FIVE:

Living

A Life

Of Integrity

Day 29

ARE YOU SHARING GOD?

"And do not forget to do good and to share with others, for with such sacrifices God is pleased."
Hebrews 13:16

DAILY PRAYER

God, I love you. I am so busy. Few things make me more uncomfortable than publicly sharing you with my friends. I feel very guilty, and please help me overcome this. Lord, I want to share your name with everyone. I love you, Jesus.

Many Christians are afraid of the idea of sharing their faith. Jesus never intended for the Great Commission to be an impossible burden. He meant for us to be witnesses of Jesus Christ through the natural outcome of living for him. We often make evangelism very complicated. God designed an easy evangelism program and made it simple for us.

Represent Jesus in the Best Possible Way. Try to keep in mind that you are the face of Jesus to the world. As followers of Christ, the quality of our witness to the world carries eternal implications. Unfortunately, Jesus needs to be better represented by many of his followers. None of us are perfect followers of Jesus; however, if we could represent him authentically, the term "Christian" or "Christ-follower" would be more likely to elicit a positive response than a negative one.

Be a Friend by Showing Love Jesus was a close friend to hated tax collectors like Matthew and Zacchaeus. He was called "Friend of

Sinners" in Matthew 11:19. If we are his followers, we ought to be accused of being a friend of sinners too. Jesus taught us how to share the Gospel by showing our love to others."Love one another. As I have loved you, so you must love one another. By this, everyone will know that you are my disciples. If you love one another." (John 13:34-35) Jesus didn't quarrel with people. Our heated debates are not likely to draw someone into the kingdom. Titus 3:9 says, "But avoid foolish controversies, genealogies, arguments, and quarrels about the law because these are unprofitable and useless."

Be a Good, Kind, and Godly Example When we spend time in the presence of Jesus, his character will rub off on us. With his Holy Spirit working in us, we can forgive our enemies and love those who hate us, just as our Lord did. By His grace, we can be good examples to those outside the kingdom who watch our lives. The Apostle Paul taught young Timothy, "And the Lord's servant must not be quarrelsome but must be kind to everyone, able to teach, not resentful." (2 Timothy 2:24) One of the finest examples in the Bible of a faithful believer who won the respect of pagan kings is the prophet, Daniel. Daniel so distinguished himself among the administrators that the king planned to set him over the kingdom. At this, the administrators and tried to find grounds for charges against Daniel in his conduct of government affairs, but they could not do so. They could find no corruption in him because he was trustworthy and neither corrupt nor negligent. Finally, these men said, "We will never find any basis for charges against this man, Daniel unless it has something to do with the law of his God." (Daniel 6:3-5)

Submit to Authority and Obey God Romans chapter 13 teaches us that rebelling against authority is the same as rebelling against God. The only time we have permission to disobey authority is when submitting to that authority means we would be disobeying God. The story of

Shadrach, Meshach, and Abednego tells of three young Hebrew captives who were determined to worship and obey God above all others. When King Nebuchadnezzar commanded the people to fall and worship a golden image he had built, these three men refused. Courageously, they stood before the king, who pressured them to deny God or face death in a fiery furnace. When they chose to obey God above the king, they didn't know with certainty that God would rescue them from the flames, but they stood firm anyway. And God delivered them miraculously.

Pray for God to Open a Door. In our eagerness to be witnesses for Christ, we often rush ahead of God. We may see an open door to share the Gospel. Still, if we jump in without devoting time to prayer, our efforts may be futile or counterproductive. Only by seeking the Lord in prayer are we led through doors that God alone can open. Only by prayer will our witnessing have the desired effect. The great Apostle Paul knew a thing or two about effective witnessing. He gave us this trustworthy advice: "Devote yourselves to prayer, being watchful and thankful. And pray for us, too, that God may open a door for our message, so that we may proclaim the mystery of Christ, for which I am in chains." (Colossians 4:2-3)

More Practical Ways to Share Your Faith By Being an Example.
People can spot a phony from a mile away. The absolute worst thing we can do is say one thing and do another. It would help if we were committed to applying Christian principles in our own life to be effective and be seen as insincere and phony. People are interested in what we say but more interested in seeing it works in our life. One of the best ways to share our faith is to demonstrate the very things we believe by staying positive and having a good attitude, even in the middle of a crisis in your own life.

Don't compromise your beliefs. Situations happen every day where compromise is possible and often expected. Show people that you are living a life of integrity. The ability to forgive quickly is a compelling way to show how Christianity works. Become a model of forgiveness. Nothing creates division, hostility, and turmoil more than an unwillingness to forgive the people who hurt you. Of course, there will be times when you are right. But being right doesn't give you a free pass to punish, humiliate, or embarrass someone else. And it most certainly doesn't eliminate your responsibility to forgive. Matthew's Gospel tells us that Jesus cared for the people He taught. The Lord looked at them and saw helpless people—like sheep without a shepherd. Matthew tells us that Jesus responded by telling His disciples;

"The harvest is plentiful, but the workers are few. Therefore, ask the Lord of the harvest to send workers into his harvest field."
Matthew 9:37–38

We, too, should pray for workers to help bring in the harvest. But like the disciples, we should recognize that we are those workers. The prayer for harvesters is that our hearts would be open and ready to respond to God's leading. Remembering we're not being told to create converts; we're asked to share the good news. It's God who will turn people's hearts. God's commission is to grow and expand His Kingdom worldwide, meaning we're missionaries everywhere we find ourselves. We must often work on losing valuable relationships and avoiding the tensions accompanying these discussions. Sometimes, we also need to be more equipped. We want to share more, but we're scared we'll field questions or deal with objections that are too uncomfortable to handle.

Fear is the common thread that weaves many responses regarding why we are not sharing Christ. You may have used words like "fear," "scared," or "afraid" to describe your feelings about other reasons we don't talk about spiritual matters. Many of these fears evaporate when we realize that a person's salvation isn't dependent upon our performance. God is at work in everyone's life, drawing them to Him. Our small conversations are part of that process. You might initiate that final dialogue that God uses to encourage them to trust Jesus. Still, more often than not, your conversation will be one the Holy Spirit uses to soften their heart. Paul addresses this when he tells the Corinthian church, "I planted the seed, Apollos watered it, but God has been making it grow. So neither the one who plants nor the one who waters is anything, but only God, who makes things grow." (1 Corinthians 3:6–7)

The ideal moment seldom presents itself. Sometimes, the circumstances never seem right. While several legitimate reasons might limit our opportunity to share His faith, this is often a problem associated with expectations. We are usually hoping for a clear signal that a moment is perfect. We might expect a certain feeling of inner peace to come when the time is right. Or it could be that we're waiting for someone to say, "Hey, could you tell me more about what you believe?" And while this happens on occasion, sharing our faith is a skill that requires trial and error. We can learn to recognize, seize, or even create opportunities, but it's a skill we develop through prayerful practice. First, we must devote ourselves to prayer, being watchful and thankful. Second, we should pray that God may open a door for our message so that we may proclaim the mystery of Christ. Pray that we may declare it. Third, we must be wise in our actions toward outsiders and make the most of every opportunity. "Let our conversation be always full of grace, seasoned with salt, so that we may know how to answer everyone." (Colossians 4:2–6). Amazing things happen when this kind of zeal is mixed with prayerful discernment.

More than once, Jesus sent His disciples out to share the good news with surrounding villages. Preparing His followers to do the work of evangelism was a high priority. He knew that eventually, He'd give them the Great Commission and send them into the world as His witnesses. We must recognize the importance of preparing Christians to share our faith. This means equipping them through training and teaching. But it also means encouraging and preparing them to trust God and step out in faith. Ultimately, God will use our imperfect efforts, and it's through practice that we grow in confidence. Your evangelism partner might be sitting in your study group with you this week.

Some don't believe they have the time to share the Gospel. In their mind, evangelism is potentially time-consuming, and their lives are busy enough. Too often, busyness is a way to excuse things we have not prioritized. We must consider several things when we're tempted to justify ourselves as too busy to share our faith. First, we must ask ourselves if we're using busyness as a cover for apathy. We all have the same amount of time, and we find time for important things to us. We also need to ask if we have faith that God can give us the time to do His work. The pace of modern life is crazy, but we must make time for the critical work of expanding the kingdom. Most people do evangelism as they go through their typical day. They're demonstrating the love of Jesus and looking for (and creating) opportunities to share their faith.

In Paul's writings, he indicates that some people have a unique ability to share the good news. They tend to be extroverted and enjoy talking to others about Jesus. And while there are people for whom evangelism comes naturally, we're all called to do our share. It's OK that you don't feel comfortable knocking on a stranger's door to talk about Jesus—God does not call everyone to do that. Some are uncomfortable talking about their faith with others. It feels like a high-stakes conversation. If you're shy, you should choose your opportunities carefully but not make introversion an excuse to keep the good news to yourself. If someone was ill and you knew how they could get life-saving medicine, you wouldn't allow shyness to get in the way. We need to have faith that the benefit of knowing Jesus outweighs our discomfort.

"For God did not send his Son into the world to condemn the world, but to save the world through him."
John 3:17

Several people don't want to share their faith at work or feel that relationships need a healthier place to talk about Jesus. These concerns are valid, as most work environments aren't the best place for these conversations. Employers don't want their employees to feel uncomfortable at work. Faith-based discussions can lead to people feeling harassed or even filing hostile work environment claims. But this helps us recognize that many Christians feel there's no appropriate time to share their faith because they're far from many non-Christians. After being a Christian for a while, many people's social circles have mainly become Christian-centric. There are only a few places where they interact with folks who don't share their faith. So, for many, work is the only place they interact with non-Christians. The answer isn't that people need to feel more comfortable proselytizing at work. Instead, Jesus would be better served if more Christians found ways to expand their circles beyond other Christians. If we're modeling our lives after Jesus, we'll find ways to invite others into our circles.

"Neither do people light a lamp and put it under a bowl. Instead, they put it on its stand, giving everyone in the house light. In the same way, let your light shine before others, that they may see your good deeds and glorify your Father in heaven."
Matthew 5:15–16

How do you steer a conversation toward Jesus? This is the question many people struggle with. It can feel tricky to segue a discussion toward faith issues without making it feel forced and awkward. Witnessing can be very uncomfortable if we don't know how to do it well. Trying to make this transition feels so unpleasant that people abandon sharing their faith altogether. The problem is that we often consider faith a topic that people need to be more interested in or has no practical value. Listening and asking questions are keys to bringing up religion naturally. The transition will always feel forced when focused on turning a conversation into an evangelistic opportunity. But when genuinely interested in getting to know others and learning about their story, we discover natural opportunities to share the good news.

"Preach the word; be prepared in season and out of season; correct, rebuke and encourage—with great patience and careful instruction."
2 Timothy 4:2

No one likes to feel cornered and badgered. Empathetic Christians tend to feel genuine concern about putting others in a frustrating or embarrassing position. The problem arises when we project uncomfortableness on others before talking to them. There's a massive difference between being bold and being pushy. The difference lies in our ability to read others. We want to pay attention to opportunities while gauging people's receptivity. This helps us recognize when to engage and when to back off. Learning to listen effectively takes some work, which comes through practice. Sometimes, we must be willing to do it poorly to know how to do it effectively.

"Yet to all who did receive him, to those who believed in his name, he gave the right to become children of God."
John 1:12

Notes From Reading:

Questions For The Group:

Prayer Request for Today:

Day 30

WHAT DO YOU STAND FOR?

"Good people will be remembered as a blessing, but the wicked will soon be forgotten."
Proverbs 10:7

DAILY PRAYER

God, I love you. I want to be remembered as a person who loved you more than anything else in my life. When I look at my time, that will not show this. Help me leave a legacy that you will be proud of, and so will my family. I love you, Jesus.

You may think that standing up for Christ involves preaching on street corners, traveling as a missionary to far-off countries, or debating your atheist friend at work. However, standing up for Christ begins much closer to home. First of all, it begins with a personal confession of faith. Romans 10:9-10 says, "*Because if you confess with your mouth that Jesus is Lord and believe in your heart that God raised him from the dead, you will be saved. For with the heart, one believes and is justified; with the mouth, one confesses and is saved.*" Those who believe in and receive Jesus Christ as Lord and Savior are declared righteous before God, not because of their righteousness, but based on the righteousness of Christ. So, we might say that standing up for Christ begins with us standing before God, our justification. To stand up for Christ, we must first believe in Him.

Standing for Christ involves the pursuit of personal holiness. Although we are declared righteous in God's sight based on the righteousness of

Christ, we are also called to grow in Christ daily. This ongoing process of being conformed to Christ's image and likeness is called sanctification. Standing up for Christ without pursuing personal holiness is nothing but hypocrisy. Even though Christians will never reach experiential perfection (glorification) until after death (Philippians 3:20-21), it is our great privilege and responsibility to pursue and grow in holiness now continually.

"Strive for peace with everyone, and for the holiness without which no one will see the Lord."
Hebrews 12:14

1 Peter 1:15-16 says, "But as he who called you is holy, you also be holy in all your conduct since it is written, 'You shall be holy, for I am holy.'" To stand up for Christ, we must seek to be holy and holy like Him. Standing up for Christ means loving others and doing good to them. However, loving each other is one way to show the world we are Christ's disciples. Jesus told His disciples, "By this, all people will know that you are my disciples if you have a love for one another." (John 13:35) To stand up for Christ, we must love the body of Christ, which is made up of our fellow believers. Standing up for Christ involves proclaiming the truth of the Gospel boldly and unashamedly.

"And he said to them, 'Go into all the world and proclaim the gospel to the whole creation.'"
Mark 16:15

Paul wrote in Romans 1:16-17, "For I am not ashamed of the Gospel, for it is the power of God for salvation to everyone who believes, to the Jew first and also to the Greek. For in it the righteousness of God is revealed from faith for faith, as it is written, 'The righteous shall live by faith.'" To stand up for Christ, we must share the good news about Him with the world.

Standing up for Christ means being patient and prayerful toward those who oppose Him and us. 2 Timothy 2:24-26 instructs, "And the Lord's servant must not be quarrelsome but kind to everyone, able to teach, patiently enduring evil, correcting his opponents with gentleness. God may perhaps grant them repentance leading to a knowledge of the truth, and they may come to their senses and escape from the devil's snare after being captured by him to do his will." To stand up for Christ, we must also pray for those who oppose and persecute us. (Matthew 5:44-48) Standing up for faith in an anti-Christian world means living a life of faith with intentionality and integrity. We must first know Christ and then strive to be like Him, recognizing that this work is only accomplished through the power of the Holy Spirit. We should treat others with love and respect. And we must share the truth with those who don't yet know Christ, praying that God will soften their hearts and draw them to Himself. Finally, we pray for God to work in us, bringing us to completion (Philippians 1:6) and giving us strength and courage to stand in Him.Standing up for faith cannot be easy when so many oppose us. But we know that "suffering produces endurance, and endurance produces character, and character produces hope, and hope does not put us to shame, because God's love has been poured into our hearts through the Holy Spirit who has been given to us." (Romans 5:3-5)

"Count it all joy, my brothers, when you meet trials of various kinds, for you know that the testing of your faith produces steadfastness. And let steadfastness have its full effect, that you may be perfect and complete, lacking in nothing."
James 1:2-4

Christians in America are under fire. We are accused of being racist and judgmental and blamed for being hypocritical; how should those of us who follow Jesus respond? According to the media, people claiming to be Christians rail against immigrants, Muslims, liberals, the media, and others who may believe, behave, or look differently than they do. They seem to endorse white nationalism or remain silent in the face of such evil. Some seem to be afraid of America's changing demographics. Some feel they must "fight to protect their Christian culture." There is a distinct difference between cultural Christianity and those of us who have chosen to surrender our lives to follow Jesus. Followers of Jesus should follow in the footsteps of Jesus. How did He oppose the pagan and religious culture of his time and bring lasting change? He sacrificed his life in an expression of love. Jesus invites us to "take up our cross daily" - die to self and live by faith. We should not be surprised that people without faith would choose to live differently than what the Bible describes. When the world opposes the high standard we see in the Scriptures, we should not let fear guide our words and actions. Instead, we must live as the Bible describes to influence the world and make a real difference. The Bible reminds us who we are in our world, to whom we should share our allegiance, and how to bring genuine transformation.

Amid a time of persecution and even when victimized by an evil empire, Peter encourages those who follow Christ to remember that we are citizens first of another Kingdom, even as we should honor those in authority. He writes: "Dear friends, I urge you, as foreigners and exiles, to abstain from sinful desires, which wage war against your soul. Live such good lives among the pagans that, though they accuse you of doing wrong, they may see your good deeds and glorify God on the day he visits us." (1 Peter 2:11-12)

Jeremiah says, "*You can be satisfied and content even in exile!*" *He also says*, "Be a blessing to those around you—even those who oppose you!" We should be the absolute best Americans we can be as neighbors, citizens, government officials, or whatever our vocation may be.

"For I know the plans I have for you, declares the Lord, plans for welfare and not for evil, to give you a future and a hope. Then you will call upon me and come and pray to me, and I will hear you. You will seek and find me when you seek me with all your heart."
Jeremiah 29:11-12

Many of us love this passage! We love that God has hopeful plans for us! But, at the same time, most of us may not realize this passage was written to people who lived in exile. They had lost their homes. Some had lost family members or friends due to the policies and decisions of the Babylonians. But, even still, God called them to make a positive difference in their homes. They were to make the most of where they lived. Scriptures remind us that, ultimately, as people of faith, our allegiance is first and foremost to the Kingdom of God. So naturally, we represent Jesus everywhere we go, including online, at work, at home, in a nation with a Christian heritage, or in a place where persecution remains the norm. The world should know that we care for them as broken as they may be, yet we are against the evils of racism, bigotry, white nationalism, and injustice. Unfortunately, our silence has been perceived as an endorsement. Our unwillingness to acknowledge the sins of our nation's past makes it seem like we agree with injustice continuing. Jesus forgives us because we were willing to repent, so we should be the first to repent on behalf of our country because of the evil perpetrated on people who look differently. It is to Him we look for peace and security.

Too often, Christians make a person's stance on political issues a litmus test for whether a relationship can develop. As a result, if people don't believe as we do, we push them further and further away, diminishing our ability to influence other Christians with different values and those who do not claim to follow Christ. Instead, we should examine each issue independently of any particular political party and then dialogue with those who often disagree with us. Some politicized evangelicals criticize other Christian leaders for specific points on which they agree with liberals, and some more progressive Christians do the same toward conservatives. This implies that we should avoid all contact with others unless they agree with us in every way. If we took this approach, the pool of people we could network or partner with would dwindle to a small puddle.

During the Civil Rights movement, Martin Luther King, Jr. once said: "The Civil Rights Act was expected by many to suffer the fate of the Supreme Court decisions on school desegregation… massive defiance. But this pessimism overlooked a factor of supreme importance… this legislation was first written in the streets." The Civil Rights Act leveled the playing field for many, but laws do not change people's hearts. Standing up for faith in an anti-Christian world means living a life of faith with intentionality and integrity.

Notes From Reading:

____

____

____

Questions For The Group:

____

____

____

Prayer Request for Today:

____

____

____

Day 31

GIVE EVERYTHING TO HIM

"Before him, no king like him, who turned to the LORD with all his heart and soul and with all his might, according to all the Law of Moses, nor did any like him arise after him."
2 Kings 23:25

DAILY PRAYER

Jesus, please help me learn how to trust you when I am over my head, honestly. I want to give you my life: the good and the bad. I am given more than I can handle, so please help me. There is nothing that you don't know about me, so you know that I try to solve everything myself. You are like none other than Jesus.

Most of us don't particularly like others telling us what to do, so when we talk about giving our problems up, we sometimes feel that we *"can't handle our problems."* The truth is, we can't. You are not alone if you think this way. Often, we don't talk about our problems because we don't want others to know about our business. It sometimes seems so simple to say, *"I'm giving my problems to Jesus."* He wants this from us and expects that we shouldn't continue to worry and carry our troubles around once we give them to Him. After giving our problems to Jesus, we should feel free; however, we only hedge our bets while overcoming our problems ourselves. When was the last time you had a big problem? You may need money in the bank account and a $1,000 car repair bill that needs to be paid. Your air conditioning is out and home, and it's 98 degrees outside, or you have tuition due and no money to pay for it. Worse yet, your spouse has just been diagnosed with a significant health issue. We all remember these types of big problems. When we realize an issue is too much for us to continue bearing on our own, we remember that we should ask for God's help. Is it your first thought when problems come calling or your last resort?

Making such a decision is excellent, and it is the first step in giving our lives over to God, but it certainly isn't the final step. When we give something over to God, it's not a one-time occurrence. Although we might be able to look back and point to a specific moment when we decided to give an issue over to God, there is hardly an exact time when you can ultimately say, "I left it all with God then and there." Sometimes, God miraculously cures people of their addictions, suffering, vices, or whatever else plagues them. But often, healing through God requires going on a journey with Him through our issues. Giving something over to God is not like flipping a light switch. But sometimes, we treat it like it is. We expect only the most miraculous healing and don't recognize and appreciate the incredible love God has to offer us in worldly temptations and silent struggles.

Why do we worry so much? Jesus says: *"If you then are not able to do the least, why are you anxious for the rest?"* (Luke 12:26) God can do everything, but we can't even do the least. In light of this truth, we should, quite logically, start being obedient to this verse: *"... casting all your care upon Him, for He cares for you."* (1 Peter 5:7). To do this, we must have a personal relationship with Him. Only His disciples have this kind of relationship—those born again to a living hope. If you are without God and hope here on earth, it isn't easy to cast all your care on Him. Instead, you become worried, and with good reason. By faith in God's Word, entire mountains of anxiety can be toppled and cast into the depths of the sea. Your thoughts tumble around, and the same destructive thoughts continue repeatedly. But, when we cast all our burdens on the Lord, heaven opens up. So, let us exercise ourselves in casting all our cares and anxiety on Him. Without a doubt, this is one of the most profitable *"spiritual activities"* we can practice.

"Do not be anxious about anything, but in every situation, by prayer and petition, with thanksgiving, present your requests to God. And the peace of God, which transcends all understanding, will guard your hearts and minds in Christ Jesus."
Philippians 4:6-7

I heard about a man who spent nights worrying and couldn't sleep. He thought about this verse: *"He who watches over Israel will neither slumber nor sleep."* He said, *"Well, Lord, we don't need to stay up all night. I'm going to sleep."* The Bible says, *"You will keep in perfect peace those whose minds are steadfast because they trust in you."* (Isaiah 26:3). On the one hand, we must pray earnestly, but on the other, get some sleep. It may be time to turn your problems over to Him. Heap them on the Lord. It doesn't matter how big or small they are; he can handle your concerns. When we obey God, peace will master our anxiety. Truly resting in the Lord is one of the most challenging things for us. We often think He may need my help. We must learn and accept that life was never meant to be lived in our power, strength, or wisdom. Oh, if it were that easy! Worry is a constant battle for most people. Worrying can lead to high anxiety, which can trigger physical illness. Worrying can harm your health, making you tired, stressed, speed up the aging process and sometimes more prone to depression. Many sermons have also stated that fear is the opposite of faith. The opposite of faith is fear, hope, despair, and love, indifference. Fear is the "*default mode*" of the soul that dwells in darkness.

As Christians, we are called to walk by faith, not sight. We are to believe first, and then He shows us the reality of who He is and the validity of the situation. God always seems to give us the test first so we can then learn the lesson! The Bible provides us with this command concerning worry, *"Be careful for nothing; but in everything by prayer and supplication with thanksgiving let your requests be made known unto God."* (Philippians 4:6) The word *"careful"* also means anxious or worried. We have discussed that worry causes high anxiety, can trigger illness, causes tiredness and depression, speeds up aging, and is the opposite of faith. The Bible says we shouldn't do it! So, how do we stop worrying, or at least worry less? It does no good to worry about tomorrow because we may not have tomorrow. If we are worried about tomorrow's problems, we often miss out on the blessings of today. Most of us worry unnecessarily about many things. We search for problems to stress ourselves out. The fantastic news is that much of what we worry about doesn't matter! Take a look at these statistics about worry:

- 40% of all things that we worry about never come to pass
- 30% of all our worries involve past decisions that cannot be changed
- 12% focus on criticism from others who spoke because they felt inferior
- 10% are related to our health, which gets worse when we worry
- 8% of our worries could be described as "legitimate" causes for concern

Isn't that remarkable? Fewer than one "problem" in every ten that we worry about is a genuine concern. All others are things that we can learn to see differently or eliminate. God does not wish for us to spend our days worrying, not about the future, our children, our health, our money, or anything else. Instead, he will provide for all who have trusted and believed Him. Worry has been defined as *"a small trickle of fear that meanders through the mind until it cuts a channel into which all other thoughts are drained."*

"Therefore, I tell you, do not worry about your life, what you will eat or drink, or your body, what you will wear. Is not life more important than food, and the body more important than clothes?"
Matthew 6:25

Here are some reasons why we should not worry. The same God who created life in you can be trusted with the details of that life. We are the most valuable of all God's creatures. In all that we face, we can trust God – even in bad times. But we must choose to let go of our worries and trust him. I think that is why Matt Redman writes that he will say, *"Blessed be your name."*

Blessed be Your name,
When the sun's shining down on me
When the world's "all as it should be."
Blessed be Your name
Blessed be Your name,
On the road marked with suffering
Though there's a pain in the offering
Blessed be Your name
… You give and take away
My heart will choose to say
Lord, blessed be Your name.

"Look at the birds of the air; they do not sow, reap, or store away in barns, yet your heavenly Father feeds them. Are you not much more valuable than they?"
Matthew 6:26

Worrying about the future hampers your efforts today. Go outside and look up at the birds. They don't care what happens. God is in charge of you.

"Who of you, by worrying, can add a single hour to his life?"
Matthew 6:27

Worrying is more harmful than helpful. In a wise tale, death was walking toward a city, and a man stopped death and asked, *"What are you going to do?"* *"I'm going to kill 10,000 people today,"* death said. The man ran ahead to the city. He warned everybody he passed that death was coming and what he would do. He again met death. He said, *"You said you were only going to kill 10,000 people, and now 70,000 are dead,"* death said, *"I killed only 10,000. Worry and fear killed the others."*

"And why do you worry about clothes? See how the lilies of the field grow. They do not labor or spin. Yet I tell you that not even Solomon was dressed like one of these in all his splendor. 30 If that is how God clothes the grass of the field, which is here today. Tomorrow is thrown into the fire; will he not much more clothe you, O you of little faith?"
Matthew 6:28-30

God does not ignore those who depend on Him. We may worry about things, but we have much to be thankful for to God. If we have food in the refrigerator, clothes on our back, a roof overhead, and a place to sleep, we are richer than 75% of this world. If we have money in the bank, in our wallet, and spare change in a dish someplace, we are among the top 8% of the world's wealth. If we woke up with more health than illness this morning, we are more blessed than the million who will not survive this week. Suppose you have never experienced the danger of battle, the loneliness of imprisonment, the agony of torture, or the pangs of starvation. In that case, we are ahead of 500 million people worldwide. If we can attend church meetings without fear of harassment, arrest, torture, or death, we are more blessed than three billion worldwide. And if your parents are still alive and married, you are very rare, even in the United States.

"So do not worry, saying, `What shall we eat?' or `What shall we drink?' or `What shall we wear?' For the pagans run after all these things, and your heavenly Father knows that you need them."
Matthew 6:31-32

Worrying shows a lack of faith and understanding of God. When faith conquers our worrying, we need to have a child-like faith. A child does not worry all day long whether his house will be there when he gets home from school or whether his parents will have made dinner. In the same way, Christians should trust God to supply what is best for them.

"But seek his kingdom and righteousness first, and all these things will also be given to you."
Matthew 6:33

Worrying keeps you from focusing on what God wants you to pursue. There are two kinds of people in the world. The "Can-dos" and the "Will-dos." Everyone can do something, but only some are willing to persevere, sacrifice, and be willing to do something. So stop worrying about what you think you can do and focus on what you will do.

"Therefore, do not worry about tomorrow; tomorrow will worry about itself. Each day has enough trouble of its own."
Matthew 6:34

Living one day at a time keeps us from being consumed with worry. It does no good to worry about tomorrow. We may not have it tomorrow. If you are worried about tomorrow's problems, you will miss out on today's blessings.

Notes From Reading:

____

____

____

Questions For The Group:

____

____

____

Prayer Request for Today:

____

____

____

Day 32

DON'T COMPROMISE

"it is a ,So whoever knows the right thing to do and fails to do it for him
.sin"
James 4:17

DAILY PRAYER

God, I love you. Sometimes, I should be less judgemental and more flexible. Then there are times when I feel I am compromising on things I know you do not want me to compromise. Please help me be strong and see the difference between the two. I love you, Jesus.

All people, whether Christian or non-Christian, feel the lure to compromise. Dr. Bryan Chapell, president of Covenant Theological Seminary, tells a true story of one individual's resolve not to compromise her faith. Karen worked full-time to keep Randy, her husband, and a seminary student in school and food on the table. In addition, Karen worked as a quality control inspector for a major pharmaceutical company. One day, at Karen's work, a large order of syringes became contaminated and, therefore, failed her inspection. When Karen reported the problem to her boss, he quickly computed the costs of reproducing the order. Then, he made a *"cost-effective"* decision. Despite the contamination, he ordered her to sign the inspection clearance. Because of specific federal regulations, only Karen could sign the clearance forms. The syringes could only be sold if she signed the documents. Karen refused to sign the papers. Even though her boss threatened her, Karen would not budge. The impasse between Karen and her boss led to a visit from the company president. He also computed the costs and told her the forms needed to be signed! Karen would have the weekend to think over her decision. It was made very clear that her job was now in jeopardy. Much more than Karen's job was in jeopardy. You see, her career was this couple's only means of support. Randy's education and their family's future were now in danger. All their hopes, dreams, and career plans of many years could now be shattered due to a choice to be made in only two days. For this young couple, all the theological jargon about living an obedient Christian life came down to this very concrete decision: could they compromise and remain undefiled before God?

"Watch and pray so that you will not fall into temptation. The spirit is willing, but the body is weak."
Matthew 26:41

This couple's predicament is similar to what God's people have faced in all ages. There have always been pressures on believers to compromise their obedience to God. If we are serious about living an obedient Christian life, we can count on facing multiple pressures to compromise. An employer will pressure some of us. Friends or relatives will pressure others. Then, there is the internal pressure that comes from our natural desires. Finally, there are the pressures of getting ahead, a promotion, a large contract, an "A" on an exam, and so on. Such forces confront anyone who seeks to live uncompromisingly for the Lord in this generation.

One of life's significant challenges is to remain diligent and not compromise. It's so easy that once life starts and you experience some seasons of success, just put things on cruise control. Have you been there before? After 12 years of building Jerusalem's commerce, culture, and community, the leaders slowly drifted from their vows, promises, and passionate pursuit of God. This is how spiritual drift usually occurs: it's not an intentional act or some big decision. Instead, it is just a tiny step in the opposite direction followed by another small step and then another. Compromise happens one degree at a time. And before we know it, we have compromised our faith and values, threatening everything we are. We become like the boxer who is exhausted and drops his hands. When you drop your hands, you've dropped your guard, and that's when you become vulnerable. Unfortunately, that's what happens to a lot of us. We're treating life's journey as a sprint rather than a marathon, and we wear ourselves out, causing us to drop our guard. Time drifts by, and with it, we slowly begin to drift one small step at a time from our commitment to God and to place Him first in our lives.

"Do not set foot on the path of the wicked or walk in the way of evil men. Avoid it, do not travel on it; turn from it and go on your way."
Proverbs 4:14-15

This is the way it is with compromise. What seems to be an innocuous situation soon has tremendous implications. Many of you started strong; you had great potential, passion, and purpose, but you've dropped your guard. You've dropped your guard in your marriage. You've dropped your guard in your careers. You've dropped your guard in your parenting. You've dropped your guard on your finances. And whenever you drop your guard, you reap the consequences of your compromise. Subtle compromise will have tremendous results as it grows and affects every area of your life. It's like the old saying, *"If a rat can get its nose in a hole, it will get its whole body in eventually."* Suppose you make a small compromise today, and a more significant settlement will follow. In that case, you will reap the fruit of sin tomorrow. To sin means to miss the mark. Missing the mark is caused by subtle compromises.

"My son, if sinners entice you, do not give in to them."
Proverbs 1:10

Compromise impacts not only us but others, too. We live in a relativistic society. People no longer believe in absolutes. Nothing is wrong with everybody, which means I can do whatever I want as long as it doesn't hurt anybody else. But the fact is our lives are a web of relationships. And what happens to me impacts the people in my life. It is vital to re-evaluate our associations to keep from lowering our guards. They may start innocently, but they will eventually influence you for good or ill. What's keeping you from doing the work of God and pursuing his life dream for you? The people in our lives can either bring out the best in us or they can bring out the worst. They can lift us to our purpose or drag us down. Paul warns us, *"Do not be misled: "Bad company corrupts good character."* (1 Corinthians 13:33) If you find yourself hanging out with evil, ultimately, you will find yourself sleeping with the enemy.

"He who walks righteously and speaks what is right, who rejects gain from extortion and keeps his hand from accepting bribes, who stops his ears against plots of murder and shuts his eyes against contemplating evil—this is the man who will dwell on the heights, whose refuge will be the mountain fortress. His bread will be supplied, and water will not fail him."
Isaiah 33:15-16

Any time you take the initiative to pursue God's purpose or advance the Kingdom of God, expect evil and opposition so you won't be blindsided. That means you must always be on guard and still work to keep your guard up. One key to keeping your guard up is Paul's advice in Ephesians 6:11: *"Put on the full armor of God so that you can take your stand against the devil's schemes."* In other words, be prepared and expect evil and opposition. We must avoid small compromises. The little things can cause us to do wrong even when we have the right intentions. The little things cause us to turn our backs and set us on the path of spiritual drift away from God. When you begin to compromise your integrity, it will hinder God's ability to use and work through you to accomplish his will. The power of God works best in your life when you live a life of integrity in God.

"And do not give the devil a foothold."
Ephesians 4:27

It is crucial to set up a system of accountability. So many of us have to live with the repercussions of our compromises because we've been trying to live for God by ourselves. Even Jesus sent the disciples out two by 2 to support one another and hold each other accountable in their lives and actions. When we try to live for Jesus ourselves, we're not living as God intended. We can't do this by ourselves! That's why we need the body of Christ for support and accountability. You and I need people in our lives who will hold us accountable. Who holds you accountable? Who reminds you of your promises and tells you how you're doing?

"No temptation has seized you except what is common to man. And God is faithful; He will not let you be tempted beyond what you can bear. But when tempted, He will also provide a way out so you can stand up under it."
I Corinthians 10:13

We may be unable to stop the opposition or limit evil's advances toward us. Still, we can choose to have the courage to correct what prevents us from pursuing our life purpose. So many want to do great things for God, but we need the courage to accomplish that. And here's the promise of God: "*I will give you power.*" (Acts 1:8) We are called and equipped to work in and through the power of God.

God is looking for warriors, not wimps who will speak and call out evil by name. Our silence makes you just as guilty as the perpetrator. One of the biggest threats to justice and curbing crime in our community is people unwilling to witness crimes they have seen. Nationally, there is a campaign called "*Stop Snitching.*" This campaign convinces informants and witnesses to stop "snitching" or informing law enforcement. Some public officials and others say criminals use a drive to frighten people with information from reporting their activities to the police. It is our calling to speak out against evil and injustice. We are called to be the voice of God. We are not better than anybody, but we must call evil by name and confront it. God says you can't be controlled by intimidation, but you need courage for that to be the case. We must speak out against the things that stop us from fulfilling our life purpose and establishing the Kingdom of God here. Sin has little power over our lives when we have the right priorities. When you realign your preferences, then God is on your side. "*I gave orders to purify the rooms, and then I put back into them the equipment of the house of God, with the grain offerings and the incense.*" When we realign our priorities and realize it is not about us but about honoring God, God's house won't be neglected. When you realign your priorities, God is celebrated, and you get in a position for God to use you. Right now, where you are sitting, it doesn't matter what you have done or what promises or vows you might have compromised on; God has not forgotten about you. God is ready to use you for a greater purpose. God will give you grace right now to be a greater blessing. God will give you strength not to compromise or lower your guard again. God wants to do some powerful things through ordinary people like you to restore hope to those in despair. May we never compromise on the task at hand or the will of God for our life together.

We hear that word compromise in politics, and it is a good thing. Recently, media personalities asked: "*When will the Republicans and Democrats reach a compromise so that we can move forward together?*" Compromise: It sounds like a good thing, at least in politics. What about compromise in relationships? Compromise in marriage is not only essential; it is necessary. Think of couples shopping together, and you'll understand the importance of compromise. Some shop slowly like they're leading a group of children on a field trip. There is minimal attention span, many bathrooms, and snack breaks, and generally, you move about .5 miles an hour. On the other hand, in a mall, the spouse moves like a Navy Seal team on a rescue op. It's an in-and-out mission--we've got to make the clothing extraction. They are running in, almost at a frantic pace, checking the sign to find the location of the store they need; then, they map out the most strategic route to find the fastest shortcut, and they are in the store and out with jeans in about 18 seconds. The cashier is thinking, "Did you see something?" So when a couple goes shopping, they must use "compromise." One has to slow down, and simultaneously, the other has to speed up. As a result, they both compromise their strategies and enjoy their life and marriage much better. In politics, relationships, and business agreements, compromise is essential. But in our moral and spiritual lives, when we use the word "*compromise,*" this is a very negative thing.

Tony Evans says compromise is the cancer of the Church, and we must rid Christ's body of it. While Christians can compromise on preferences, they cannot compromise on principles. We can't be one way on Sunday and another on Monday. This is a major problem among Christians in America today. We don't take a stand. We don't keep our standards. We merely shift to satisfy society. Compromise has been a constant temptation ever since Satan convinced Adam and Eve to reinterpret God's Word his way. Compromise teaches that we don't need to obey God completely. Instead, we can pick and choose what *we* think is right. We can follow the world or do whatever we want.

Today, we must listen to the warnings. Remember that the world seeks to deceive you with clever words, lures you with desirable rewards, and urges you to reject God and His Word. But if you want success, commit unwittingly to obeying God and His Word. Love Him and seek an intimate, personal relationship with Him. Trust Him. Have faith in Him, and avoid compromising.

Notes From Reading:

____

____

____

____

Questions For The Group:

____

____

____

Prayer Request for Today:

____

____

____

DAY 33

LEAVING A LEGACY

"Do not store up for yourselves treasures on earth, where moths and vermin destroy, and where thieves break in and steal. But store up for yourselves treasures in Heaven, where moths and vermin do not destroy, and where thieves do not break in and steal."
Matthew 6:19-20

DAILY PRAYER

Jesus, I have little to leave regarding a legacy. Some so many people have done such great things. Use me, starting today, to build the legacy that you created for me to make.

Why are we so concerned about leaving a legacy? What type of legacy do you want to leave for your family? For some, our legacy writing journey is further down the road. For others, the reality is this: most of our lives are now viewed through the rear-view mirror. If that is true, and your legacy is something you would like to redo, remember, *"The mercies of the Lord are new every morning,* "and you can start right now, this day, re-shaping your legacy. We know that we are all going to die. Some of us have barely started the game of life. Some of us are in the third quarter of the game. Others are in the fourth quarter, yet some are still in overtime. We usually think we aren't ready to die when reminded of our death — we want to live longer! But we understand death's inevitability, which creates a dilemma in light of our profoundly rooted survival instinct. One of the most significant things we can do to buffer our death anxiety is to attempt to transcend death by finding something that will make the world remember us.

Central to this meaning is that we have an impact that persists beyond our physical existence. The epitome of power is to leave a great legacy that lives on after we are gone. This is how you can maximize your influence and keep the long-term in mind. Ultimately, some believe that our legacy is all we have. Think about how you want to be remembered by other people and act on those thoughts. Then, give the Grim Reaper a run for his money by creating something meaningful that will outlive you. Many of us have been blessed to live in a family that has provided us with Godly examples in our grandparents, parents, aunts, and uncles. I am thankful for the Godly people in my family who shared their spiritual legacy with me. I have also benefited from the Christian legacy in my spiritual family at my Church left by many faithful members who lived in the past and some who still live today. We should all be in the legacy-building phase of our life. We know that three generations after our death, we will be just a faceless name on a sheet of paper; however, we want to pass on our legacy of Christ. (Proverbs 13:22) *"A good man leaves an inheritance to his children's children."* Even more than striving to bestow a material inheritance, we should make leaving a rich spiritual legacy one of our top priorities.

How can we leave our family a Christian legacy that stands the test of time? First, we can live in such a manner that God's Word and commandments are on our hearts. They will become interwoven into everything that we are and all that we do. We must share the Bible with our family. The truth of Scripture will significantly impact your children and grandchildren more than any material you can give them. The truth of God's love for us and the reality of Christ's love for us will light a fire of faith that cannot be quenched. And we should model true Christianity by living a Godly life. Bringing the Bible to life is much more memorable than just speaking words.

What do you want to leave your loved ones when you are gone? Money? Things? Legacy? When Jesus finished His time here on earth, He decided on what to leave His disciples—the peace of God. *"Peace I leave with you; My peace I give you."* Peace does not come easily these days. So many things cause pressure in our lives that push out our peace. Our nerves are frayed. We cannot relax. We are restless, worried, and irritable. The burden and demands of work, money, the guilt of sin, the fear of sickness, and sometimes the fear of living. These wear us down. Christ offers us His peace. He provides us the same serenity with which He had gone to Golgotha. He calms our troubled hearts with the same peace that stilled the Sea of Galilee and the fear-filled hearts of His disciples. He grants the same peace He breathed on His apostles when He commissioned them, *"Peace I leave with you."* He grants the peace of a clean heart and a right spirit, the peace of guilt removed. Sins are forgiven, and the peace of fellowship with God gives us strength for every burden and sufficient resources for every task. The peace of God passes all understanding. Nothing can disturb it.

We often desire to be smart enough to grasp the meaning of Scripture each time we read it. But, sometimes, we don't, so we dig deeper into the word until we say, *"WOW, now I get it."* Today's verse may be one of those. You have read this verse for years but may have recently understood it. To help us understand, an authentic shepherd once provided insight into this verse. He pointed out that much of the Psalm's significance is lost unless we know the problems of a shepherd in Bible times.

One of his stimulating verse-by-verse explanations ran as follows: *"Preparing a table does not mean setting a dinner table indoors, but refers to the shepherd's chief concern, finding a proper feeding place for his flock. He must constantly look for poisonous gases, for his sheep do not always know the difference between healthy and death-bringing plants. His ever-watchful eye must detect snakes lying in ambush and drive them off. All this requires unceasing vigilance. Then, after finding a good patch of healthy grass free from snakes, the shepherd must render it safe "in the presence of enemies." There are jackals, wolves around the feeding ground in holes and caverns on the hillside, and hyenas bent upon destroying the sheep. So the shepherd builds an enclosure of rocks and slays them with his long-bladed knife if the wild beasts attempt to enter the enclosure."* This single verse alone in Psalm 23 indicates what infinite care God takes to protect His children night and day.

> *"How joyful are those who fear the Lord and delight in obeying his commands? Their children will be successful everywhere; an entire generation of godly people will be blessed."*
> *Psalms 112:1-2*

What kind of legacy will you leave? Will it last? Will it be imperishable and eternal? Or will you leave behind only tangible items—buildings, money, or possessions? The Apostle Paul instructed Timothy in (2 Timothy 2:2) to *"...teach these truths to other trustworthy people who will be able to pass them on to others."* So, what are you passing on to the next generation?

How does God want you to invest the time you have been given in the day-to-day grind of life? We all have the potential to get caught up in life's hectic details and demands. As a result, we can quickly lose sight of whether we are leaving a Godly legacy to our children. Leaving a Godly legacy is our purpose as parents. In (Exodus 20:6), God tells Moses: *"But I lavish unfailing love for a thousand generations on those who love me and obey my commands."* What we do matters because it can affect generations. When we as parents understand that what we do today affects how our children remember their childhoods, mold who they are, and see life, we get serious about making changes that create a Godly legacy.

"Don't wait in ambush at the home of the godly, and don't raid the house where the godly live. The godly may trip seven times, but they will get up again. But one disaster is enough to overthrow the wicked."
Proverbs 24:15-16

Everyone has an inner desire to succeed. This desire can be strong, and we can sometimes become very competitive. We want to run faster, jump higher, and endure longer. We want to make more money, have more stuff, and leave a more lasting legacy. We want to succeed as Christians as well. We set goals, and we hope for great things. We want to make significant contributions to the Kingdom. But there are often things in our lives we would like to change for the better to be a better Christian.

Today is the perfect jumping-off point to put hope into action. We all want to improve our flaws, such as not spending enough time with our children, becoming better parents, holding grudges, gossiping, or even addictions. But here is the thing: "I tried to address my area that needed improvement last year and failed." What if I fail again? It's too painful to fail, so I will not get my hopes up. Many people look at failure as being final. But as the old saying goes, it is not over until it is over. Your life is over once you stand before the Lord Jesus Christ. Until then, it is not over. Until it is over, it is not over. We have all had failures. We have all made mistakes in our life.

"And when thy son asketh thee in time to come, saying, 'What mean the testimonies and the statutes and the judgments which the Lord our God hath commanded you?' Then thou shalt say unto thy son, 'We were Pharaoh's bondmen in Egypt, and the Lord brought us out of Egypt with a mighty hand... And He brought us out from thence that He might bring us in."
Deuteronomy 6:20-23

We're going to leave a legacy. Besides your relationship with God, your family is an essential thing in your life. The best thing most of us can do is ask, *"Oh, God, teach me how to walk in victory. Lord, get me out of this wilderness. I want to be a Spirit-filled Christian living in victory."*

Notes From Reading:

Questions For The Group:

Prayer Request for Today:

Day 34

ARE PEOPLE COUNTING ON YOU?

"Are not two sparrows sold for a penny? And not one of them will fall to the ground apart from your Father. But even the hairs on your head are all numbered. Fear not, therefore; you are of more value than many sparrows."
Matthew 10:29-31

DAILY PRAYER

God, I love you. So many days, I feel like I have the whole world's weight on my shoulders. There is so much pressure to raise a family and provide that I am failing. I know you are with me, Jesus, but I need your guidance and help. Help me to lean on You and stop trying to do everything myself. I love you, Jesus.

Who's counting on you? Have you ever thought about it? Who's counting on you for support? For hope? For love? For Christ? Do you remember when the NBA Hall of Famer Charles Barkley told the press that he wasn't a *"role model and no one should count on him"*? He thought Whether you feel it or not, many are counting on you whether you see it or not. Someone is counting on you for:

- Encouragement.
- Security
- Listen.
- Introduce them to Jesus.

According to the dictionary, to be dependable means *"to be capable of being depended on, suitable or fit to be relied on, worthy of one's trust, good, reliable, responsible, safe, solid, steady, sure, tried-and-true, trustworthy, trusty."*

Let's look at the picture of a dependable friend in (Ecclesiastes 4:9-12). *"Two are better than one because they have a good return for their work: If one falls, his friend can help him. But pity the man who falls and has no one to help him up! Also, if two lie down together, they will keep warm. But how can one keep warm alone? Though one may be overpowered, two can defend themselves."* People can count on you to serve. *"Two are better than one because they have a good return for their work."* In the Good News Bible, it says, *"...because together they can work more effectively."* Then, in the Contemporary English Version, it says, *"...because then you will get more enjoyment out of what you earn."* In short, together, we can do things easier, faster, and better. To be reliable means that people can count on us to do so when we are asked to help.

"You obey the law of Christ when you offer each other a helping hand."
Galatians 6:2

The Bible says: *"A friend loves at all times."* I like how the Contemporary English Version translated it. *"A friend is always a friend..."* Here, we see that one of the traits of someone you can count on is that they are dependable. They have staying power no matter what happens. (Proverbs 18:24) declared: *"A man of many companions may come to ruin, but there is a friend who sticks closer than a brother."* There are currently about eight billion people in the world. We're a metaphorical speck of dust in an infinite universe. But you are essential, and people count on you. You matter. What does that mean for you right now as you read this chapter? It means that who you are and what you do matters to more people than you can imagine. You affect the world around you in a myriad of ways. Think of the law of cause and effect. Your thoughts, words, and actions bring a ripple effect into the world around you. The ripple affects people and things you're not even aware of. Whether you know it or not, people are counting on you. You also have the potential to contribute value to the world around you. In this sense, you cannot only change yourself, but you can also make the world a better place. The fact that you are alive is a miracle. Millions of sperm cells didn't survive the journey, but you did. Life is a gift, but temporary because we will all die one day. This is why it behooves us to do something worthwhile while here. Our life is a canvas in a frame. The frame is the world and circumstances you were born into. You had no control or say in those. But the canvas is you. Your thoughts, decisions, and actions. However, these are the things we have control over, and we can paint some of our pictures. We have infinite possibilities about what we can do or have. The life we've chosen isn't what we must have tomorrow, next month, or next year. If we can't see your importance, no one else will. We need no reason to acknowledge our importance other than we are alive.

People who live fulfilling lives are those with a primary purpose to live for. What's yours? You can have what you want when you decide exactly what that is and commit yourself to work for it. You have a unique set of characteristics, interests, and abilities. The world is such a large and diversified place that there is a place for you. Follow your interests and hone your abilities to the point that the world needs who you are. Ask yourself what people are counting on you for.

"God is not unjust; he will not forget your work and the love you have shown him as you have helped his people and continue to help them."
Hebrews 6:10

We all have a variety of life experiences. These experiences mean we've been through what other people have yet to experience. Being able to share knowledge, wisdom, and experience with other people is a gift. With you, they have access to the information. You can share your experiences with a neighbor or write books for millions of people. In both scenarios, you're making a positive contribution. People need you. If you don't have an experience worth sharing, think again. We discount ourselves because we don't consider ourselves exciting or essential. But we are. People don't see you as you see yourself. The people who love you see qualities in you that you're not even aware of. You have a lot more to offer than you think. People need you. Having goals and objectives implies you're a focused person. A high percentage of people need clear goals or objectives. Even if there are things they say they want, they do nothing about it. When you have clear goals that you're pursuing, you affect your own and other people's lives. The attainment of the goal is important but not the most important. It's secondary to the attempt and the journey. From when you set a goal to the moment you achieve it, you change and evolve in many ways. You're important because you're working towards your goals and objectives. You're not sitting on your couch, lazy and unproductive. That should be applauded. Give yourself credit where it's due. Pursue your goals and objectives with nonstop action. Keep going until you have what you want because people count on you.

"And do not forget to do good and to share with others, for with such sacrifices God is pleased." Hebrews 13:16

You can love and appreciate the people around you. It's a comforting feeling to know someone cares. You can give someone that gift. The best way to make others feel special and loved is to share a little of yourself. The words *"You're special, and I love you"* and show it through your actions are two different acts. Some people love and care about you dearly. You are important to them. If you weren't here, they would miss you. Sometimes, it takes a smile or a brief acknowledgment to make someone's day. You can make others feel good and have a positive energy about them. You get to choose what type of person you are. This doesn't mean you walk around giving hugs to strangers, telling them you love them (although you could). It means you show genuine love and appreciation to the people that matter to you most. Wherever people are in life, they can always be more, do more, have more, and give more. It's a personal choice. This chapter is about you and why you are essential. Remind yourself in times of doubt that you matter and that people count on you. How can you contribute more to yourself and the world around you? Why do people seem to need you? Do you want others around you to lean on you more often when they need help? Of course, our ultimate job is to point people to Jesus when they need help. However, we also know that many people cherish and enjoy having people rely on us for support.

Do people trust you? Do they believe in you? Do they want to follow you? If the answer is yes, you have people counting on you. Being someone who is being counted is often difficult. While we love having those who need us occasionally, it comes with the pressure of not letting them down.

> *"Every good and perfect gift is from above, coming down from the*
> *Father of the heavenly lights, who does not*
> *change like shifting shadows."*
> *James 1:17*

Several things go to the pressure of having people count on us. First, it's all a matter of doing what we said. When we say that we will do something, we do it. When we say we will get the job done, we do the job. When we say that we will show up, we're there. So you will be counted on when you keep your word. Even though people are counting on us, we are imperfect. We're going to fail. And people are going to see it. So, what do I do when I fail those counting on me? The answer is still simple. When we fail, we apologize and tell those who count on us that we failed. First, you tell them that you made a mistake. Then you tell them that you're going to fix that mistake in the future and that you're going to get back up. Then we show them.

If someone asked you what one of your best qualities was, could you say that being an individual can count on one of them? Well, if you are, you know how hard being reliable can be. But, when your family goes through things, they know they can count on you. They can rely on you to be a listening ear, lend a helping hand, or support them in their endeavors. So they call you to vent, request, extend an invitation—whatever their heart desires.

A friend recently marked a significant milestone in her life. She invited a few friends and family to celebrate that milestone. She sent out info about how she planned to celebrate a week in advance. She wanted to spend time with some of her favorite people, including her family and called about eight or nine loved ones. On the day of her event, only two friends showed up. The rest, including family, either canceled on her, waited until after the event to text her, or ignored her text message altogether. Or, worst of all, they said they would come and then failed to show up, let alone send a message explaining why they suddenly went MIA. She tried to smile that evening but eventually shared her pain with me. *"I'm just really disappointed that I got stood up by people I'm always there for,"* she said. *"I would never do them like that."* And therein lies the problem.

Her family knew that. Her friends knew that. And that's why they feel comfortable enough to disappoint her. When you know someone doesn't have the heart to disappoint others; you can always count on them to show up. That's why people are so disappointed with individuals known for having a good track record when they fall through. They're less than surprised by those who always bail on others.

"Carry each other's burdens, and in this way, you will fulfill the law of Christ."
Galatians 6:2

You've been there. People ask you to watch their kids, pick them up, let them stay in your place, take on extra responsibilities, etc. They know you're dependable and probably won't find the same excuse everyone else they thought of calling would have come up with. And so, you dutifully give and give of yourself, even when it's a significant inconvenience. This is one of the sacrifices of being a giving person, someone others count on. You don't give because you want the kudos or because you only want someone to know they owe you. You give because you know whatever you could do was the right thing to do. You also understand that by blessing someone else, you will be blessed. And the more you're blessed, the more responsibility you have to give.

Notes From Reading:

Questions For The Group:

Prayer Request for Today:

Day 35

WHEN NO ONE IS LOOKING

*"Teaching them to observe all that I have commanded you. And behold,
I am with you always, to the end of the age."*
—Matthew 28:20

DAILY PRAYER

God, I love you. I am sometimes alone, and no one is watching. Whether traveling or at home. Please protect me, Jesus, as there are places my mind wants me to go that I know you don't want me to be. I can't do this by myself. I am tempted at every turn. Keep me close and surrounded by the Holy Spirit. I love you, Jesus.

Have you ever seen those reality TV shows that expose people's actions when they're not being watched? You know, the show calls in four plumbers to do a job, and one of them puts in a little more work than the others trying to fix a leak in the kitchen and the bedroom. But, then, what the plumber thought he was doing secretly is suddenly broadcast. To protect him from embarrassment, though they do pixelate his face. In this age of technology, no one is safe, not even you, because you never know when you're being watched. Technology can be scary because you can never know if you are being watched. So what's all this got to do with God? One of God's characteristics is that he is omniscient, which is a significant way of saying he knows everything. Like the hidden camera, the hairs of your head, your future, your past, and he knows what you do when you think no one is watching.

This may make some feel uncomfortable. Maybe the thought of God knowing your secrets makes you squirm in your seat a little. And you may wonder who turned up the heat in this place. On the one hand, the fact that God knows everything is comforting. But, on the other hand, it's terrifying. It blows away our feelings when we do something we think no one will ever know. It's not that we were caught on tape, but God knows all things. It would not be all bad news; if it were, we would run to the hills. But we know we wouldn't be the only person looking for a hole to hide in. We would be following in some pretty essential footsteps. If ever there was someone who should despair over this being caught out, it's a guy called David. King David. David wasn't caught on tape like the plumber trying to fix a leak in the women's underwear drawer. But records of what he did are in the Bible. He's the guy who saw this girl called Bethsheba taking a bath one day and set up her husband so that he would be killed in Battle. If ever there was a person who should worry about God's ability to see all, it should be him. And yet, he doesn't seem too worried. He delights in God, knowing him intimately.

Why does David not run and hide from this God who knows his darkest secret? Why doesn't he bury himself in some lead-lined box, hoping God cannot see? Firstly, even back then, there was something called forgiveness in the Old Testament. David knew a lot about it because he made many public and private mistakes. But there's something else; it goes down to how God reacts to our secret sins. Jesus was tempted in every way we are and did not give in to desires or sin. Yet, this same Jesus could look upon a crowd and pity them, even though a crowd called out for him to be killed. Jesus knew then and knows now about all our secret little sins, yet he doesn't turn his back. He doesn't seek to scandalize us by putting our blacked-out faces on national TV and calling in entertainment.

Knowing what we do in secret drew out his compassion for us. But there's another side, too, because if we can't keep any secrets from God, why do we try to hide from it? One of our biggest problems is the energy we waste trying to cover up. God already knows; we can't hide it, so why try? Rather than wasting our time covering up, why don't we just come clean, admit it to God, and move on? But this gets me about the whole thing: despite what we do, God still loves you.

Several years ago, I heard what is likely nothing more than an "*Urban Legend*," one of those stories that get passed around as if it had happened. Still, something about this one makes me wish it were true. According to the story, a man was driving down the interstate and saw a stranded limousine on the side of the road. He's running late on his way home from work, so he drives by. But then, he starts thinking about how, if he were having car trouble, he would hope that somebody would stop to help him, so he pulls to the side of the road, walks up to the driver's window, and offers his cell phone. The driver says his phone wasn't working, so he gratefully accepts. As the driver called for help, the limo's back window rolled down, and an older man stuck his head out to thank the man for his assistance and to ask if there was anything that he could do for him. The man tells the man that the best thing he could do would be to send his wife flowers because she would never believe he was late getting home. After all, he had stopped to help someone in a limo. The man said he would do just that and took the man's wife's name and address. The following day, the doorbell rang. The wife answered the door to find a gigantic flower arrangement with an attached card that read: "*Thank you very much for the help. I took the liberty of paying off your mortgage.*" The next time you see a limo on the side of the road, you'll stop. The man in the story did not have to stop to help the limo that night. He didn't know he was going to get a reward. He knew that the right thing to do was to stop and help, so he did that.

Each of us has to decide daily and sometimes hourly – Will I do what I know is correct? And the answer to that question is enormous because it clarifies who we are. Someone said our character is defined by who we are when no one looks. It's not the same as reputation – what other people think about us. No, a character is who we are. That's character. Now, the obvious question is, do we want to have a Godly character or not? Most of us would say, *"Of course we do!"* The problem is, while it's relatively easy to have Godly character while we're around others who are Godly, it can be challenging to be Godly when we're around those who aren't or when we're by ourselves in our private moments. Few of us commit heinous sins on Sunday mornings at Church because we know everybody's watching. But what about when we're away from the Church, at home, at work, or alone? Do we go off our *"best behavior"* and make choices that we know dishonor God? Still, we make them anyway because they seem like they'd be fun or advantageous to us, and besides, nobody from the Church will ever know.

It could be how we treat people. It could be what we say to hurt others or the type of language we use. It could be books we read, magazines we look at, movies we watch, or what we view on the internet. Whatever it is for each of us, most face the regular temptation to compromise our godly character.

"Train yourself to be godly."
1 Timothy 4:7

Train yourself – the original Greek word is gumnadzo, from which we get our English word gymnasium. The word meant "to exercise naked," which was how ancient Greek athletes exercised. But here, the term is being used figuratively to indicate that Christians must train inwardly, where they are naked before God. Others may not see, but God does. Even on the inside, we're naked before Him. So, in our most inward, personal, private lives, we are to exercise ourselves and train ourselves to be godly. And it's not just that we do it once, and then we're done with it. The form of the verb used here is a present imperative, which in the Greek language indicates that you keep on doing it. In other words, we keep on training ourselves to be godly. Now, the word *"Godly"* describes a manner of life, born of faith and lived in such a way that God is honored, and others are confronted with His truth as they see us striving for holiness. It suggests we are trying to be God-like, with God's characteristics: love, faith, purity, generosity, and kindness. *"Godly"* doesn't mean that we are perfect. It means that we are struggling for perfection, that we are doing our best to live lives that are pleasing to God, honoring Him, and convicting others.

"For physical training is of some value, but godliness has value for all things, holding promise for both the present life and the life to come."
1 Timothy 4:8

Here, Paul acknowledges that physical exercise does some good. It helps you slim down and improves your health. It has some value. But someday, we will still die; it's not of eternal value. But spiritual training, producing Godly lives – that has value, Paul writes, for all things, because it holds forth a promise for this life – that is, that we will have a clear conscience and know that we're honoring God. We'll draw others to Him because of our conduct. It promises this life and the future – we'll live forever in Heaven!

So, how do we do it? How do we train ourselves to be Godly? How do we develop a Godly character that stays true to God, even when away from the Church or ourselves? Is Satan tempting us to compromise our faith and do things or say things we know are wrong? First, we must make a spiritual commitment.

"I have taken an oath and confirmed it that I will follow your righteous laws."
Psalm 119:106

The writer is talking about a spiritual commitment to be Godly. Without that type of commitment, our Godliness will be hit-and-miss at best. That may seem obvious, but you would be surprised at the number of Christians who have never really committed to Godly living. There are some Christians who, when they hear sermons about Godliness, think, "Yeah, the minister's right. We should live better!" And then they leave the Church that morning without ever committing to God that they will start living better! And without that type of commitment, they fall when temptation arises. They return to Church the following Sunday, wondering what's wrong with them and why they give in to sin so easily. And we know why – they haven't committed to being any different.

"Submit yourselves, then, to God. Resist the devil -- now, that's key! -- resist the devil, and he will flee from you."
James 4:7

We've got to commit! We've got to submit to God and say, "God, I want to live my life in a way that honors you!" And then, when the devil brings temptation, having that type of commitment will help us resist him! It's just like physical exercise or dieting. You've got to commit to doing it, or else you will only do it briefly. It's painful sometimes, and there are other things you could be doing that would be more fun than going to work out for an hour or two. But, if you're going to be serious about physical fitness, you've got to commit. You've got to say to yourself, "I'm going to do this!" It's the same with spiritual training. You've got to commit yourself to God, "I want to be Godly all the time!"

Some Christians mean well, but they've never made that commitment. They want to do better and don't understand why they always seem to fall prey to the same old sins, but they still need to take the first step! There are other Christians who are going through the motions of Christianity. Their motto is, "I love to sin, and God loves to forgive, so this is a win-win relationship!" They're not even trying, and they're not concerned about it at all. They're confident that they're saved, within God's grace, and training themselves to be Godly seems like a real downer they don't need. They don't realize the peril they're putting themselves in. While the Bible makes plain that we are not saved on account of what we do but rather because of what Christ did, it also says that those saved will live godly lives! James even goes so far as to say in his letter in the Bible that we are justified by what we do, not by faith alone, and that faith without works is dead.

"Not everyone who says to me, 'Lord, Lord,' will enter the Kingdom of Heaven, but only he who does the will of my Father who is in Heaven."
Matthew 7:21

If we want to be Godly, we've got to know God; we can only do that by spending time with him! Actors and actresses understand this principle. What do they do when they play the part of a natural person still living? They try to spend time with that person to speak and act as that person would, bringing that character to life on the screen! It's the same way if we want to be Godly. If we want to do the things that please God and develop the characteristics of God, we've got to spend time with God. The people I admire most for their godly lives have been deeply committed to prayer and Bible reading.

"I have hidden your word in my heart, that I might not sin against you."
Psalm 119:11

You may have heard, "Integrity is doing the right thing, even when no one is watching." But research has repeatedly shown that people are more honest when they know they're being watched. You are being watched every second. Are you accountable for what you say is your truth? Do you walk your talk –whether or not you're being watched?

Notes From Reading:

____

____

____

____

Questions For The Group:

____

____

____

Prayer Request for Today:

____

____

____

WEEK SIX:

How Will You Allow Jesus To Use You?

DAY 36

USING YOUR GIFTS

*"Each of you should use whatever gift you have received to serve others
as faithful stewards of God's grace in its various forms."*
1 Peter 4:10

DAILY PRAYER

*Lord Jesus, I want to do your will. I want to discover what you created
for me and what you have called me to do. Please help me identify my
spiritual gift and help me use it for Your glory. I know the things I am
good at, but allow me to know if that is the gift you placed in me before I
was born.*

God has a purpose for you. He made you for a purpose and gifted you to
accomplish that purpose. Our goal is to discover that dream and live it.
But it would help if we found "it" first. God's plan for us is hardwired
into who He made us to be. He wrote that dream in our heart and in who
we are. Your spiritual gifts is to be used to serve in a specific way that
blesses the body of Christ—knowing our spiritual gifts release us to
function in our God-given place of service. The apostle Paul made this
clear when he wrote in his letter to the Romans: "For as we have many
members in one body, but all the members do not have the same
function, so we, being many, are one body in Christ, and individually
members of one another. Having giftedly differing according to the
grace given us, let us use them: if prophecy, let us prophesy in
proportion to our faith." (Romans 12:4-6) The search for spiritual
gifting has become an incredible frustration to many people. Most of us
think we know what we are good at, so we don't stop long enough to

determine what gifts God placed within us for His glory. Though the Bible is clear that spiritual gifts are essential, it is strangely silent on how to discover those gifts.

Do you remember when you wanted to learn to drive a car? Maybe your Father had let you sit in his lap and steer the vehicle several times, but that was not good enough. You wanted to sit behind the wheel by yourself. Someone had shown you how to shift the gears and how to steer. Now you were ready to "solo." But did you have the guts to try it? The crucial test was whether or not you would take what you had learned and put it to use. More than discovering and developing your gifts are required. The moment comes when we must demonstrate action- get up before people and speak or share the gospel with someone orally. Always present is the danger of failure and the possibility of error. But we must take the risk if we are to use our gifts.
Also, we must understand that just because we don't see certain people in the choir loft, the pulpit, or serving on the deacon board or teaching a Sunday school class, that doesn't mean that God does not gift the individual to do those things. You may never see the person sing, preach, or teach. Still, that same person can cook in a kitchen, fix broken things, draw beautiful pictures, open and operate a business, build houses, work with young people, coach or play sports, do secretarial work, etc. We should never look down on people who may not have the same gift that we may have. Whatever gift God has given us is for us, and whatever gift God has given to somebody else, it is for them. Instead of being jealous of one another, we should work together with our God-given gifts for a common goal. That common goal is to glorify Jesus Christ with whatever gift God has given us.

The Bible teaches that every Christian has at least one gift. This spiritual gift differs from our natural ability. Everybody has natural skills, but only believers have spiritual gifts. Romans 12:6-8 says, "We have different gifts, according to the grace given to each of us. If your gift is prophesying, then prophesy per your faith; if it is serving, then serve; if it is teaching, then teach; if it is to encourage, then give encouragement; if it is giving, then give generously; if it is to lead, do it diligently; if it is to show mercy, do it cheerfully." God chooses the ones you are going to get. They are given by grace—you don't earn the gift. It is just God's gift to you. Scripture teaches us that "There are diversities of gifts, but the same Spirit. There are differences of ministries, but the same Lord. And there are diversities of activities, but it is the same God who works all in all."(1 Corinthians 12:4-6) Your spiritual gifts determine how God wants you to serve Him. Once you understand your spiritual gift, it answers many questions for you. What is God's will for your life? What does he want you to do now that you are a Christian? What should be your ministry? How should you spend your time? All of these questions begin to be answered when you understand your gift. Every Christian is called to serve Christ's cause, but your spiritual gift shows how you are to serve Him particularly. If you are gifted to organize, God wants you to be an organizer. If you are gifted to teach, you need to be a teacher. If God has gifted you with music, you should be in some music ministry. Finally, if you are gifted in reaching people for Christ, you must witness evangelistic ministry. Every gift in your life is unique. You are not to try to copy other people's spiritual gifts. God doesn't want you to copy anybody else. You need to be the best "you" to glorify Jesus Christ. He knows the gift that is best for you. That is why He chooses it. Gifts explain why Christians who believe the same thing see things differently. If you are gifted in evangelism, all you can think about is reaching non-Christians. You can only think about discipleship if you are gifted in teaching and growing people. If you are gifted in mercy, you focus on helping hurting people. Some have the gift of giving. They enjoy giving to causes that help advance Christ's Kingdom.

Is your spiritual gift serving others? A researcher from Harvard recently tracked the lives of 7,000 people over nine years. The results fascinated both the researcher and his team. The most isolated people (people with few relationships) were three times more likely to die early than those with healthy relationships. People with solid friendships but lousy health habits (such as smoking, obesity, or alcohol) lived significantly longer than those with excellent health habits but were isolated. Christian author John Ortberg said, "In other words, it is better to eat Twinkies with good friends than to eat broccoli alone." I love this guy. The point is this--we need to use our time and resources to serve others the best we can with the gift God has given us. We desperately need service—a place to give back just a portion of what we have been given. It may only be calling someone or emailing them asking them how you can help. When God had created stars, plants, fish, and birds—every time He made something, He'd say, "That's good." And when He created Adam, God declared that he was "very good." But then, after He created Adam, God said: "It is not good that the man should be alone." (Genesis 2:18) We can only share our gifts if we focus on being around people. Unfortunately, some believe Christians serve others less than they did a couple of decades ago. It is not good that a person should be alone. That's why Jesus created the Church. Ephesians 5:25 says, "Christ... loved the church and gave himself up for her..." And Jesus died to establish the Church, in part, to have a place where we could be with other Christians, build friendships, and serve others.

I was fortunate to have one of the last private interviews with the admired legendary NCAA basketball coach, John Wooden. I spent four beautiful hours talking with the legend about his life and faith in his small apartment in California. When we had finished talking about his ten NCAA basketball championships and all the famous players he had coached, he spoke of the people in his life who had made him the man he was. He noted that he was fortunate to have Godly friends to talk with him in times of trouble and men who called and kept him accountable. He stressed that basketball was easy; finding the right people to surround yourself with to improve yourself is much more difficult. His answer surprised me when asked about the most valuable advice he'd ever given his players. He said, "Put your socks on correctly." I chuckled before he explained that his players weren't smoothing the wrinkles around their toes and heels, which caused blisters. He also made sure his players laced up their sneakers correctly and wore the right size of shoes and socks. Now, his comment made sense. Because he couldn't coach a team to victory while they sat on the bench with blisters on their feet. Coach Wooden indicated that he believed his greatest gift was his ability to see the minor things that would significantly impact people's lives. He noted that this didn't seem like such a special gift, but it had meant the world to him, his family, and his teams.

"Now, about the gifts of the spirit, brothers and sisters, I do not want you to be uninformed. You know that when you were pagans, somehow or other, you were influenced and led astray to mute idols. Therefore, I want you to know that no one who speaks by the Spirit of God says, "Jesus be cursed," and no one can say, "Jesus is Lord," except by the Holy Spirit."
1 Corinthians 12:1-3

A common approach to finding our spiritual gifts is to examine ourselves, discern our God-given strengths and abilities, and dedicate these gifts to service in God's Kingdom. That sounds simple. Many have taken a Spiritual Gift Inventory assessment that can be taken either online or by a counselor. One mistake we often make is to equate natural gifts with spiritual gifts. Most of us have things in our lives that are gifts that were evident from birth. People can use these things for good or evil, as we have seen throughout history. The fact that such inclinations, tendencies, or talents are present does not make them spiritual gifts. At best, we call them providential gifts. God, in his general providence, has permitted such talents to be present and developed. This does not constitute spiritual giftedness. A key to identifying your spiritual gift is being called by the spirit to a particular task or service area. In Biblical times, God gave Moses direct and clear revelation in Exodus 3 and Saul of Tarsus in Acts 9.

"So then, brothers and sisters, stand firm and hold fast to the teachings we passed on to you, whether by word of mouth or letter. May our Lord Jesus Christ himself and God our Father, who loved us and by his grace gave us eternal encouragement and good hope, encourage your hearts and strengthen you in every good deed and word."
2 Thessalonians 2:15-17

How did you find out that you were musically talented? Or artistically endowed? Or you able to lead, organize, or compete athletically? It probably began with some desire. You liked whatever you are talented at and found yourself drawn toward those already doing it. Many Christians today have somehow gotten the idea that doing what God wants you to do is always dreary and unpleasant, that Christians must always make choices between doing what they want to do and being happy on the one hand, versus doing what God wants them to do and being completely miserable on the other. Exercising a spiritual gift is always a satisfying experience, though sometimes the occasion it is exercised may be unhappy. Jesus said it was His constant delight to do the will of the One who sent Him.

Here is a practical, workable, step-by-step plan for discovering your spiritual gifts:

- Start with the gifts you feel most drawn toward. Then, study the biblical lists of gifts and try exercising those that appeal most to you.
- Watch for improvement and development. Do you get better at it as you go along?
- Do you find your initial fears subsiding? Remember, that's how it was to
- discover your talents, too.
- Ask trusted Christian friends to observe your life and tell you what gifts they see in you. Often, others can see our lives more clearly than we can, and they can help affirm gifts in us that we cannot see yet.

"Therefore, I urge you, brothers and sisters, because of God's mercy, to offer your bodies as a living sacrifice, holy and pleasing to God—this is your true and proper worship. Do not conform to the pattern of this world, but be transformed by renewing your mind. Then you can test and approve what God's will is: his good, pleasing, and perfect will."
Romans 12:1–2

One of the best things you can do for another Christian—and the life of the body as a whole—is to help another Christian discover their spiritual gifts. Others should affirm authentic gifts in you than for you to lay pretentious claims to gifts you might not have! One great Bible teacher used to say, "It's such a pity to see someone who thinks he has the gift of preaching—but no one in his congregation has the gift of listening!" Gifts need to be exercised just as talents do. Practice tends to make perfect, whether using talents or gifts. Paul wrote to young Timothy, "Rekindle the gift of God that is within you." (2 Timothy 1:6) As a gift develops, the spiritual blessing it brings will become increasingly evident. You will find yourself seeking more and more occasions to use your gift. But remember: that gift was not given to you for your personal, worldly advancement but as a means to spiritually enrich you and others. It is also helpful to realize that only some discover all his gifts at the beginning of their Christian experience. Like talents, Gifts may lie undiscovered for years, then emerge when a particular combination of needs or circumstances brings them to light. It is wise, therefore, to always be ready to try something new.

Notes From Reading:

Questions For The Group:

Prayer Request for Today:

Day 37

THE HOLY SPIRIT IN YOU

"But the Helper, the Holy Spirit, whom the Father will send in my name, will teach you all things and bring to your remembrance all that I have said to you."
John 14:26

DAILY PRAYER

God, I love you. Unfortunately, I have not relied on the power of the Holy Spirit as I should. It is often too much to believe when I think of You living inside me. Please help me to seek the Holy Spirit's help in every decision and every thought I have. Teach me to utilize the Spirit to help me be more like You.

When we talk about God the Father, we can understand the concept of a Father; when we talk about God the Son, again, we can understand a Son, but what happens when we say, God the Holy Spirit? Who is the Holy Spirit? He's not an it, but a person of the Godhead, and He is in every believer. The Holy Spirit does today what Jesus did 2000 years ago. Jesus' ministry on earth was to teach the things of the Father. He explained the law, showed people their sins, and comforted those who believed. The role of the Spirit in us is to remind us of the Words of Christ. He was actively doing the work of Christ and was sent by Christ to indwell believers. He lives inside of us; he cleans out the unwanted parts of us and gives power to those who allow Him to fill each aspect of their lives. We live in a challenging and complex world, and God's Spirit working in us helps us keep our footing and stand firm in our faith.

When we accept Jesus as our Savior, we receive the Holy Spirit. God's Spirit is inside every believer at all times. You don't have to experience earth-shaking "feelings" or emotions; you don't have to jump, shout, cry, roll on the floor, or display any such outward physical emotions to be indwelt with the Spirit. The Holy Spirit establishes a new relationship with us, but this is only the beginning of His work in us. First, the Holy Spirit marks us as belonging to God.

"The truth is the Good News. When you hear the truth, you put your trust in Christ. Then God marked you by giving you His Holy Spirit as a promise. The Holy Spirit was given to us to promise that we will receive everything God has for us. God's Spirit will be with us until He finishes His work of completing us. God does this to show His shining greatness."
Ephesians 1:13-14

He is our direct line, through Jesus, to the Father. He convicts us of sin and the need for righteousness in our lives. John 16:8 says, "When the Helper comes, He will show the world the truth about sin. He will show the world about being right with God. And He will show the world what it is to be guilty." He teaches us to obey the Lord, trust Him to direct our every step, and put all our cares on Him, for He is more significant than any problem. Through the Spirit, we learn to develop greater reliance on the Lord and less on human wisdom, strength, or abilities. The Spirit knows our search for truth in the visible world is futile; we must seek God's Word. He teaches us ways to see things more in-depth than what's on the surface, to help point out blind spots in our mind's eye to those areas that are not entirely yielded or fully surrendered to God. The Holy Spirit helps us to know God.

He makes us wise, reveals God to us, and helps us understand God's mind. Without the Spirit, you cannot understand God's things. We need spiritual "eyes" to see God and His ways more clearly. That's when we begin to understand God's mind, how He thinks, and how that knowledge will help us in our daily lives. The more we want to know of Him, the more the Spirit reveals to us.One of the most essential things the Holy Spirit does for us is to learn to think like God. When His Spirit takes over our thoughts, that's when things happen. Our priorities change. Before Christ, it was all about me, what I could do, what I wanted, and what I thought was best. We don't belong to ourselves anymore; we belong to God. We've been bought by a price and are no longer our own. We become better because God's Spirit is a superior influence in our lives, not because we are superior as individuals.

The Holy Spirit gives wisdom beyond our natural abilities as we learn to listen to Him. If we allow ourselves to be immersed in God and focus on His thoughts, we can do mighty things in this world. The Spirit helps us to pray. He guides us in what to pray for and how to pray. When we are committed to praying earnestly, the Spirit helps us know what to pray for and can bring God's power into the lives of those we care about through intercession. The Spirit seeks to bring greater joy to the Lord through every believer. He gives gifts to whomever He will give glory to God.

"There are different kinds of gifts. But it is the same Holy Spirit Who gives them. There are different kinds of work to be done for Him. But the work is for the same Lord. There are different ways of doing His work. But the same God uses all these ways in all people."
1 Corinthians 12:4-6

Our motivation for receiving the Holy Spirit is not to have a 'gift' but to be everything God wants us to be and not miss out on the blessings he wants to give us. The Spirit gives us the power to see God's purpose for our life. God has called us to follow Him and give us hope. That's our reason for following Him and doing what we do; how great is His power at work in us? The Bible says, *"Therefore, if anyone is in Christ, he is a new creation; the old has gone, the new has come."* (2 Corinthians 5:17) Theologians call it regeneration. We are regenerated, recreated, reborn, and changed. We are different, although we may not always feel or realize it. When the Holy Spirit fills us, our standing before God is new. We have different outlooks on life, names, directions, destinies, and Fathers. We do what he wants us to do rather than what we want to do. Our motive is to please Him rather than to please ourselves. We have a future, hope, and a place in His Kingdom, for we belong to Him. He is living within us and moves us inwardly to live for God and bring about his kingdom "on earth as it is in heaven." It is not an outward religion that motivates us; it is now an inner Person who moves us and creates an inner passion for being a part of God's plan for the world.

A person can change because we believe in the Holy Spirit. There is hope for us, and there can be a new beginning, a new power, a new you when the Holy Spirit comes into your life. The Bible says, *"Yet to all who received him, to those who believed in his name, he gave the right to become children of God — children born not of natural descent, nor human decision or a husband's will, but born of God."* (John 1:12-13) It is as simple as saying, *"Forgive me. Cleanse me. Come live in me and make me yours."* It takes all our excuses away because we can no longer say: "I want to be different, but I can't." On your own, you cannot, but with him living inside, there is nothing that you and God together cannot handle or change. No habit cannot be broken, nothing that cannot begin to be different because there is a Holy Spirit. You must realize the real power for change comes only from the Holy Spirit.

"You, however, are controlled not by the sinful nature but by the Spirit if the Spirit of God lives in you. And if anyone does not have the Spirit of Christ, he does not belong to Christ."
Romans, 8:9

All the religion in the world will do us no good, but a heart willing to admit it is wrong and in need of God will be filled with his Spirit like a cup at the bottom of a mighty waterfall. The Holy Spirit purifies us. He teaches us that we no longer belong to ourselves when filled with His Spirit. As the Bible says, "Do you not know that your body is a temple of the Holy Spirit, who is in you, whom you have received from God? You are not your own; you were bought at a price. Therefore honor God with your body." (1 Corinthians 6:19-20) Now, we belong to God, but the best part is this: God belongs to you. The Holy Spirit has created a relationship between us that is full of joy and love. It defies description. It is also true that the more we live for God, the more we realize there are parts of us that have never heard of God. We discover new things about ourselves all the time that we do not like, but they are things that we can give to the Holy Spirit and have him renew as they come up. We will never reach the perfection we desire. Still, with God as our father, our Friend, and his Spirit living inside, it is not a thing of defeat but a life of growth and victory. His Spirit shows us what we are like, and then he shows us what He is like — and what we can be. We are privileged to become more like Him, and He is patient with us in this change process. We need to recognize the presence of the Holy Spirit in each other. He is in us and will never let us go. The Bible says that the Holy Spirit seals us for the day of redemption. (Ephesians 4:30) He is not going to let us go. He will not throw us away when we make a mistake. He has the power to keep us in the family of God until Christ returns for us.

"...able to keep you from falling and to present you before his glorious presence without fault and with great joy."
Jude 1:24

The Holy Spirit can do all of this for us. He can help us to see our need for God. He can show us our guilt and relieve our guilt. He can change us, live in us, comfort us, empower us to live for him, and keep us until the Lord comes for us; all of this and more — much, much more. The Bible says, "Today if you hear his voice, do not harden your hearts." (Hebrews 3:15) Let God do what he longs to do for you. Why resist joy? Why run from peace? Only the Holy Spirit can bring you to God, and only pride can keep you away.

Pride almost kept my friend Don away. Don was a very active person in the Church. His family had been in the Church for years and held most of the offices in the Church. He sang in the choir, was a respected attorney in town, and looked on as a leader in the community and the

Church. But the day came when Don had to decide whether he would continue doing his religious duty or have a relationship with God. There was a dramatic difference when he decided to open his heart and life to the Spirit of God. Most people didn't see a change, except for his smile and softer approach to people because Don had always been a good person and active in the Church. But the difference was internal. His heart had a new peace and a quiet assurance about his relationship with God. He was captured by a new joy and motivated by a new love. His enthusiasm for God's things was catching, and he soon helped many people to come into a relationship with God for themselves. He is still leading small group Bible studies and introducing people to the One who changed his life from the inside out. Only the Holy Spirit could have prepared Don for that kind of inner change, and only the Holy Spirit could have brought that kind of rebirth. It is the same relationship that God desires to have with you. And it is yours the minute you open your heart and mind to his wonderful Holy Spirit.

Notes From Reading:

____

____

____

Questions For The Group:

____

____

____

Prayer Request for Today:

____

____

____

DAY 38

GIVING AWAY WHAT YOU DON'T OWN

"Give to the one who begs from you and does not refuse the one who would borrow from you."
— Matthew 5:42

DAILY PRAYER

Jesus, I know that everything I have comes from You. I want to help those who need it, but people everywhere need my help—not only people I don't know on the streets but also family members, co-workers, and friends. Please help me understand what I should do with my gifts and be willing to give sacrificially to those in need.

Someone is asking us for money or time everywhere we look. It is often difficult to see our hard-earned money as belonging to God. He made you, created your job, and promised to meet your needs. However, when we are in a hurry, we often need to pay more attention to many requests. We approach life with the attitude that this is my money, and I will give God his ten percent unless I have to have it for something unique. What if that was Jesus you just passed that was begging for money or your time? What if that person had fallen upon hard times through no fault of their own? While we want to ensure that our hard-earned money goes to someone who needs it, we often need to learn who is in need. Also, is our money ours or a loan from God? He wants you to take care of others. He wants you to give away what we know we can't take with us anyway. The truth is, we don't own the things we have; they were given to us by God.

We have something to offer, even if we tend to hold on to things to ensure we don't need them. We can give our money and time to charity, be a friend to someone sick or lonely, volunteer, or be peacemakers, teachers, or ministers. We may give unselfishly of our time to our spouse, children, or parents. We may choose a service-oriented occupation or do our everyday jobs with integrity and respect for others. When we are honest with ourselves, some fear that the more we give, the poorer we become. Service to others brings meaning and fulfillment to our lives in a way that wealth, power, possessions, and self-centered pursuits can never match. Today, many of us enjoy unprecedented abundance. It is easy to forget that many of the world's people live in terrible poverty. Do we have an individual responsibility to help alleviate poverty? Does the Church have a responsibility to help? Is caring for people experiencing poverty merely a good thing or a commandment from Jesus? A common theme in prayer is "Bless the poor and the needy, the sick and the afflicted, and those who have cause to mourn." Helping those in need is more than just praying for them. The desire to help others comes as a duty and through our love of Jesus Christ. There are benefits when you and I are faithful in giving to God. How does giving bring us closer to God? The Bible says, "Where your treasure is there, your heart will also be." Wherever we put our money and time, that is where our heart is. Suppose our money is in investments; that is where our heart is. If our money is in our house, that is where our heart is. If our money is in our career, then that is where your heart is. Finally, if my money is in the work of the Lord, then that is where your heart is.

"Sell all your possessions... and you will have treasure in Heaven. Then come, follow Me."
Luke 18:22

Money is like a magnet; wherever we put it, it also pulls our hearts and thoughts. Giving money to God is like a magnet; it draws us closer to God. So that means if our treasure or finances are going to God, our heart is getting closer to Him. Every time we give, it draws us closer to God. Giving is the nature and characteristic of God. Giving also draws us closer to God because giving is an act of worship, and when we worship God, it draws us closer to Him. Like we sing, praise, clap our hands, and sing worship songs, we set aside time to give because giving is an act of worship. We must remember something about money: God doesn't need our money. He owns all the silver, gold, and cattle on a thousand hills, but He wants what our money represents. When we worship God with song, words, or actions, our giving draws us closer to Him. Wherever your money is, that is where your heart is.

Sell all your stuff. Just get rid of it, all of it. That's different from what you wanted to hear on this beautiful morning. What is the most valuable thing in your life? Some might say our wife, our children, or our parents. Others list career, education, or material possessions, such as their BMW or investment portfolio. Those struggling with sickness would likely say that your health tops the list. Jesus illustrated this same question with a parable. (Matthew 13:44-46)

Our relationship with Jesus is of great value and importance; we ought to be prepared to give everything we have to follow Him and be obedient to His will. But, unfortunately, we have nothing of value that we can give God. We can't buy our way into Heaven; our salvation is "a gift from God." We can only have the treasure above if we give up our earthly treasures. The rich young ruler in Luke 18:17-24 wasn't prepared to sell all his earthly possessions to have treasure in Heaven. So he went away sad. Conversely, the young ruler knew the significant risks he took in liquidating all his assets. (Philippians 3:7-8) Missionary Jim Elliot said, "He is no fool who gives what he cannot keep gaining what he cannot lose." Jesus said, "Sell all your possessions... Then come, follow Me." (Luke 18:22)

"On one occasion, while eating with them, he gave them this command: Do not leave Jerusalem but wait for the gift my father promised, which you have heard me speak about. For John, you are baptized with water, but in a few days, you will be baptized with the Holy Spirit."
Acts 1:4-5

Just the thought of sharing the gospel with a non-Christian makes some men cringe. The feelings of rejection or inadequacy take hold of them. Many think, "I just can't do this," or "Isn't this the pastor's job?" If you are one of these people, take a deep breath and relax. The power for evangelism does not come from you—it comes from God. You are not on your own. You don't have to perform or prove anything to anyone. Let the Holy Spirit work in and through you. In Acts 1:8, shortly before Jesus ascended into Heaven, He told His disciples, "...you shall receive power when the Holy Spirit has come upon you. You shall be My witnesses both in Jerusalem, and in all Judea and Samaria, and even to the remotest part of the earth." There is no doubt that Jesus wanted His disciples to share their faith. He called them to be fishers of men. Notice, however, that Jesus wanted them to communicate when they had the power to do it effectively. Serving others means sharing the most incredible gift possible—the gospel. It may take food or lodging, but to meet these needs without sharing the gospel will have limited results. Find comfort in knowing that God never asks us to do anything He doesn't equip us for. He has prepared us to share our faith. The power to do so is not your power—it is Divine power, the power that healed the sick and raised the dead. Since God sent the Holy Spirit, every Christian has had this indwelling power. We shouldn't stress about sharing our faith. If you think you can't share, you're right; you can't. But God can do it through you because He placed His power in you. Philippians 4:13 states, "I can do everything through Him (Christ) who strengthens me."

"Do not store up for yourselves treasures on earth, where moths and vermin destroy, and where thieves break in and steal. But store up for yourselves treasures in Heaven, where moths and vermin do not destroy, and where thieves do not break in and steal. For where your treasure is, there your heart will be also."
Matthew6:19-21

In a national news story, California's Governor estimated the cost of the most recent fires in his state to be at least two billion dollars. A member of the Red Cross said, "Many who died ignored evacuation orders and were caught by flames because they waited until the last minute to flee. Because of the fire's unpredictable nature, many residents only had minutes to evacuate." Hearing the heart-wrenching stories of those who barely escaped the California firestorm should help us realize what is essential in life. Have you ever considered what you would take if you only had fifteen minutes or less to evacuate your home? All the "stuff" that we accumulate will someday be gone. We may hope that our children and grandchildren will care about some of the "stuff" we have spent a lifetime collecting, but more than likely, all may end up in a yard sale or a junk store. The Psalmist said, "Do not be afraid when one becomes rich when the glory of his house is increased; for when he dies he shall carry nothing away; his glory shall not descend after him." (Psalm 49:16-17) The spiritual reality is that only that of eternal value will last.

"He made peace with everything in heaven and on earth by means of Christ's blood on the cross."
Colossians 1:20

Suppose someone rudely swooped into that prime parking spot just ahead of you. You want to scream and throw things, but instead, you stop and say, "Well, that's just perfect. Now I can get more exercise by walking farther." This approach often helps us stop whining about trivialities. However, trying to be positive is not only difficult, but it is often impossible. In a sense, the entire Bible is devoted to showing that everything is not perfect on this earth, but it will be in Heaven.

We are commanded to give everything we have to Jesus. He is vastly more worthy of our gifts and praise than anyone or anything in our world. Unfortunately, we often get caught up in trying to obtain the perfect life here on earth. Remember, that isn't the plan and never has been. Bookending all that mayhem is a long-ago and faraway garden where the first man and woman lived in perfection and a promise that the garden's Creator will return to make everything new. (Genesis 2:1-25) And in the middle, woven into the flawed fabric of life, is a thread that gives us the reason for absolute joy—a perfect life is coming.

"There are different kinds of gifts, but the same Spirit distributes them. There are different kinds of service, but the same Lord. There are different kinds of working, but in all of them and everyone, it is the same God at work."
1 Corinthians 12: 4-6

Imagine that your favorite football team finally makes it to the playoffs. Suppose that somehow they even make it to the National Championship game. Imagine, too, they win the big game, and their quarterback is named the Most Valuable Player. During the interview, he is asked, "What do you think about winning the Super Bowl and winning the MVP?" He responds, "It is great. I can't describe the feeling. After all, I pretty much single-handedly managed to turn the team around. I was able to win games because of my superior gifts. I deserve to be the MVP

because there is no question that I am by far the most valuable player in this entire organization. If not for me, the entire team would sit at home and watch the National Championship with all the other losers."
What would you think if he said that? You would think that he is incredibly arrogant, even delusional because you know that it takes an entire team to win games. Well, this hypothetical situation was in the early Church at Corinth. The Corinthians had a skewed view of their spiritual gifts. They took personal pride in their spiritual gifts as if they had earned or deserved credit. They were much more interested in using their gifts for personal fulfillment than for the good of the church body.

Notes From Reading:

____

____

____

____

Questions For The Group:

____

____

____

Prayer Request for Today:

____

____

____

Day 39

ONE LIFE TO LIVE?

"And he said to him, "You shall love the Lord your God with all your heart, soul, and mind. This is the great first commandment. And a second is like it: You shall love your neighbor as yourself. On these two commandments depend all the Law and the Prophets."
Matthew 22:37-40

DAILY PRAYER

God, I love you. Please, Jesus, help me change my life and become more like you. I ask you to help me love my neighbor as I love myself. Lord, please use me as we end this study. I don't know how, but use me. I'm yours.

Most of us don't like to see money wasted. If someone inherits hundreds of thousands of dollars and blows it all in a few months or years, we think that's irresponsible. A 43-year-old with a wife and two children entered a local casino for the first time, just for fun, and won $10,000. Since then, he has lost about 1 million dollars. He says, "I neglected my family and friends. I lied to them and used them to get money. I blew my mother's inheritance. I lied to the banks. You do everything, anything, to get your fix." He's now suing the casino for their responsibility. It's a shame all of that happens. However, the truth for this man is that his compulsion has thrown his life out of balance. In wasting his money, he has also destroyed part of his life. Each of us has something much, much, much more valuable than a million dollars. We have time. Ask most people dying of cancer whether they'd rather have a million dollars or time. They'd rather have what you've got.

You may have much or little. But even if you have a week, you have more than some people. So, how do you keep from gambling your life away? A Nike commercial captioned, "Life is short! Just do it!" The question is, "What is 'it'?" If "it" is just bouncing around in new shoes, that doesn't seem like much. In Psalms, we find a similar statement: "Life is short; do it right."

It's the only Psalm attributed to Moses. He lived long but had some challenging experiences. This is a lament—things have not been going so well. It may have been written during the desert years before he took on leadership. It may be a mid-life Psalm. Do you remember everything that happened to you yesterday? What did you eat? Who did you talk to? Do you remember every word you said? We are limited. Our lives on earth have a morning, noon, and evening. We tend not to think about it until about noon of life. Then, some have a mid-life crisis! There's a site on the internet called deathclock.com. You can enter your date of birth, whether you smoke, your body health, and so on. It will give you a calculation of your life expectancy. Unless Jesus comes, we'll each end up with a gravestone bearing our name. That should get us thinking a little, "What on earth am I here for? How will I make the best of the time I have left?"For some, this is a frivolous question. Talk about death to a child, and she says, "Die? What's that?" To a teenager, he says, "Yeah, right, not in my lifetime." The twenty-something says, "Sure, someday." The forty crowd says, "Yikes, it's true; I'm already at half-time." Fifteen years later, there's more peace for those with faith, "That's OK; I can still live with purpose." When you're old and your body fails, you may say, "With faith in God, death is my friend." Vance Havner once said, "The hope of dying is the only thing that keeps me alive."

How long do things last? Experts estimate that if a standard DVD is played about 50 times a year, sound quality will deteriorate somewhat after nearly five years. But the disk itself will live on for years to come. A lightning bolt lasts 45 to 55 microseconds. The average running shoe worn by the average runner on an average surface will last 250 miles. A hard pencil can write up to 30,000 words or draw a line over 30 miles long. Leather combat boots have a wartime life span of six months and a peacetime life span of eight months. The projected life span of a baby born in the U.S. today is about 71 years, nearly double what it was at the end of the 18th century. The longest authenticated life span of a human being is 113 years, 214 days. In addition, studies show married people live longer than those who remain single.

"Today or tomorrow, we will go to this or that city, spend a year there, carry on business, and make money." Why do you not even know what will happen tomorrow? What is your life like? You are a mist that appears for a little while and then vanishes. Instead, you should say, "If it is the Lord's will, we will live and do this or that." As it is, you boast and brag. All such boasting is evil. Anyone who knows the good he ought to do and doesn't do it sins."
James 4:13-17

James describes the kind of attitude that Christians should have about life. The basis of our attitude, James explains, is that Christians know that they have one life to live, and it counts how you live it. How you live each day matters because we have a Savior coming back for us. How we live each day matters because tomorrow is promised to no one. In Rick Warren's book, The Purpose Driven Life, he has a chapter dedicated to Life Is A Temporary Assignment. Day six finishes Warren's thoughts about "how I see my life shapes my life." If you happened to have read this remarkable book, you would recall he said that "the Bible offers three metaphors for life: life is a test, a trust, and a temporary assignment."

The Bible is filled with teachings on the brevity of life. To make the most of life, we must realize that life is fleeting compared to eternity. We must also recognize that the earth is a temporary residence and only a staging area for eternity. We must live with a view of eternity, realizing we are an ambassador here on earth. We are only temporary residents; as Christians, our homeland is Heaven. When we have this view, we will understand why God's promises sometimes seem unfulfilled, and prayers seem to go unanswered. In the light of eternity, no promise goes unanswered and no prayer unheard, and in the end, it will all make sense. Of course, this realization should also help us place a much higher value on eternal rather than temporal factors. Warren teaches that as a fish, we will never be at home outside of water, so we will never really feel at home on earth. We will always feel discontent with life on earth because we have eternity in our hearts, and Heaven is our real home. The highlight of this chapter is the following paragraph: "In God's eyes, the greatest heroes of faith are not those who achieve prosperity, success, and power in this life, but those who treat this life as a temporary assignment and serve faithfully, expecting their promised reward in eternity." The Book of James describes this attitude toward one life to live. It is an attitude of urgency and getting priorities straight. So, let's look at what James says more closely.

LIFE IS BRIEF. The first truth that James brings to our attention is the brevity of life. The weeks fly by, and life sometimes whizzes past. James comments that we make big plans for our lives, yet we do not know what will happen tomorrow. Life is totally and unendingly unpredictable. We don't even know what will happen this afternoon! Life is brief, and we realize it is an understatement, but James makes the point. Our lives are like a mist that appears for a little while and then vanishes. We count our lives in years, but God tells us in (Psalm 90:12), our days are numbered. The truth is that we are just one heartbeat away from eternity. David comments on this in (1 Samuel 20:3), "But David took an oath and said, "Your father knows very well that I have found favor in your eyes, and he has said to himself, 'Jonathan must not know this, or he will be grieved.' Yet as surely as the LORD lives and as you live, there is only a step between me and death." David was facing an angry king and did not know what would happen from one moment to the next. David had reflected on his situation and knew his next step could be a misstep. A tragic day happened in 1963 when President John F Kennedy was gunned down. John Connally, the Texas Governor of the time, was also wounded in the gun attack. He and his wife, Nellie, were in the motorcade that day. In an interview, he said, "As far as my wife and I are concerned, this event brought into sharper focus what's important in life. We try not to participate in shallow things or, in the long run, meaningless." In other words, they felt life was too short to be caught up in meaningless things. That's probably what David had in mind in Psalm 90:12: "Teach us to use wisely all the time we have."

OUR PLANS AND GOD'S PLANS. James also comments on our habit of making plans. Now, he is not, of course, saying that we shouldn't make plans. We can plan for the holidays, events, and get-togethers. We can plan our life out. It is a wise thing to do. James is saying it is good to plan but that we need to include God in our plans. His opinion counts when it comes to decision-making and planning. As Christians, we confess Jesus as Lord and Christ… which means His will comes before ours, but we often don't live like that. We go our own way and expect God to follow. The Greek philosopher Aristotle wrestled with this issue of the brevity of life. He said, "The reasons for some animals being long-lived and others short-lived, and, in a word, causes of the length and brevity of life call for an investigation. The necessary beginning of our inquiry is a statement of the difficulties of these points. It is not clear whether, in animals and plants universally, it is a single or diverse cause that makes some long-lived and others short-lived. Plants too have in some cases a long life, while in others it lasts but for a year…."

WOULD A COULD A SHOULD. James comments on the unfulfilled things we all know we should do. We all have things in our minds that we know God wants us to do or know of some good things we can do for our neighbor. James says that we sin if we know what we should be doing and don't do it. What might cause us not to do something we know we should:

· Get distracted by our life issues (Prodigal Son)
· Get scared to do what God has said (Moses)
· We don't want to do what God wants (Jonah)
· We choose to do what we want instead of God (Adam and Eve)

James encourages us to find out what we should be doing and try to do those things while we live on this earth. An ancient philosopher once said: "One hundred years is the limit of a long life. Not one in a thousand ever attains it. Yet if they do, still unconscious, infancy and old age take up about half this time. The time he passes unconsciously while asleep at night and wasted though awake during the day also amounts to another half of the rest. Again, pain and sickness, sorrow, and fear fill up about half so that he gets only ten years or so for his enjoyment. And even then, there is not one hour free from some anxiety. What, then, is the object of human life?"

It is a question that philosophers and thinkers have been asking for centuries. What do we do with the brief time we have on this earth?

What is the purpose of man's brief existence? Why are we here? What should be our focus? The Book of James supports the truth that our life is short, and we have only a limited time to live. So what does James say should be our attitude?

- Remember that life is too brief not to have God at the center; plan with God in mind.
- Commit yourself to do God's will
- Do the things God wants you to do

So, how do you make each day count? First, we learn from God about what's worth our time. Then, we make sure we do it. A balanced spiritual life needs times of renewal. These often happen as you enjoy friendships, God's creation, or other things. Whatever the shape of your week or month, how you spend your days will determine your success. Indeed, you have the freedom to waste every day of your life. But if you want to ensure you don't gamble away your days, the formula for success may look like this. First, setting eternal priorities will place you in the right direction. The focus will keep you from getting distracted by sin and less important things. Finally, discipline will give you the ability to carry out your goals. So, for you today, where's the weak link? Are your priorities where they should be? Do they translate into your schedule? Are our particular sins distracting you and making your life complicated? How about the discipline? Accountability often helps there. I invite you to make a new commitment today, to use the time ahead to re-align your life. It could take several months. If you're a bit of a procrastinator, perhaps you can commit to praying daily about what God might do for you.

Notes From Reading:

____

____

____

____

Questions For The Group:

____

____

____

Prayer Request for Today:

____

____

____

Day 40

YOUR WALK IS YOUR WITNESS?

"But in your hearts honor Christ the Lord as holy, always being prepared to make a defense to anyone who asks you for a reason for the hope that is in you; yet do it with gentleness and respect,"
1 Peter 3:15

PRAYER FOR TODAY

God, I love you. Please, Jesus, help me change my life and become more like you. I ask you to help me love my neighbor as myself. Lord, please use me as we end this study. I don't know how, but use me. I'm yours.

What we do matters! Do we witness with our life? When we strive to be a Godly person around others, God uses our example as a testimony to them. Even if they speak ill of us, deep down inside, they know we are different. God will use your good deeds for His glory in His time. When we follow Jesus, we put ourselves on the world's biggest stage, whether we want to be there or not. We live in a culture where people aren't cheering on Christians to succeed; they look for our failures and flaws to exploit. Because of this, it is essential to live like the Jesus we claim to be following would be live. Character always communicates credibility! When we sometimes self-righteously point out others' sins while living with no higher standard, the world mocks our God. On the other hand, when we humbly walk, the world not only takes notice, but they do notice a difference in us. Our character brings credibility to Jesus and our faith! Our actions, not words, make the most significant difference! Billy Graham, one of the greatest evangelists of our time, once said: "We are the Bibles the world is reading." Someone said,

"Your life as a Christian should make non-believers question their disbelief."

Imagine you are out at the lake for a fun day and spot a person drowning. What would you do? Indeed, you would not ignore their desperate condition and turn the other way. Instead, you would throw them a life preserver or jump in to save them. I am confident you would try to do something to save the person in need. Similarly, each day, you encounter dozens of people who are desperate without Christ in their lives. It's only a matter of time for them to go down for the last time unless someone like you saves their life. One misconception we might have is that it is our pastor's or church staff's job to tell people about Christ and win the lost. The church staff are shepherds, and their prime focus, biblically, is to tend to the flock. Even if they have a genuine heart for evangelism, they can't win the entire community themselves and aren't charged to. They are to train up the church's body and equip you to go out and win the lost. Data tells us that most people who become Christians do so before age 21. Most will not just be uninvited to church and hear their pastor preach the gospel. We have a part in getting them to a place where they can listen to the Words of Jesus.

"Then Jesus came to them and said, All authority in Heaven and on earth has been given to me. Therefore, go and make disciples of all nations, baptizing them in the name of the Father, the Son, and the Holy Spirit and teaching them to obey everything I have commanded. And surely I am with you to the very end of the age."
Matthew 28:18-20

Many people are refocusing on what they believe in. You may believe in many things, such as America, Ford, Toyota, baseball, apple pie, fishing, God, Christ, the Holy Spirit, the Bible, etc. However, in times of darkness, we tend to rethink every relationship and often even what we believe. When we believe in something strongly enough, we talk about it to others at every opportunity. Many could speak all day about their hobbies and outdoor experiences. Others could tell stories about trips they have made throughout the country. Everybody has a story to tell and something they desire to share. If we are sold on something, believe in it, and are excited about it, we will share it with others because we can't keep it inside!

"It is written: I believed; therefore, I have spoken. We also believe and speak with that same Spirit of faith because we know that the one who raised the Lord Jesus from the dead will raise us with Jesus and present us with you in his presence."
II Corinthians 4:13-14

Now that you have accepted the Lord and His goodness, you should rid yourselves of bad things: malice, deceit, hypocrisy, envy, and slander. Even though Scripture doesn't say it, it seems reasonable to assume that we will also talk about the goodness we have tasted. When something is terrific in our lives, how can we not talk about it? Have we not tasted the goodness of the Lord in various ways? He gives us life, breath, and everything else. He has created us, sustains us daily, and saves us. These are different aspects of His goodness. So, how can we not talk about Him? God wants us to talk about Jesus to people because of who He is and what He did for all humanity. We don't have to be obnoxious in talking to others, but we should look for opportunities to speak a good word for Christ.

"Anyone who knows the good he ought to do and doesn't do it sins."
James 4:17

Now that we have spent forty days together sharing and studying the Words of Christ, what if we close our books, say goodbye to our new friends, and return to our previous life? This is called the sin of omission or failure to do the good we know we should. I have heard figures that say 95% of all Christians never win a single soul to Christ in their entire lifetime. If that is true, why is it true? It's probably because they never even tried to win someone to Christ! We could do many things in life if we only try! Some things may be beyond our reach, like winning the Tour de France cycling event, but we can do many things if we only try! So, what is our problem when it comes to witnessing? Why don't we do it? Several reasons can be noted.

Jesus said, "All authority in Heaven and earth has been given to me.
Therefore go and make disciples...."
Matthew 28:18

Whether we want to admit it or not, we all have an authority problem. We like to run our own lives, do our own thing, and don't particularly have others tell us what to do. However, Jesus said, "All authority in heaven and on earth has been given me….therefore you need to do what I tell you." Do you have a power problem? Do you need more power, gumption, or grit to talk to people about Christ? There have been many occasions when we have been reluctant to speak to someone about Christ. Sometimes we are so fearful. We lack the spiritual power to talk to people about Christ. How do you get that power?

"I pray that out of his glorious riches, He may strengthen you with
power through His Spirit in your inner being."
Ephesians 3:16

It is strengthened with power. Doesn't that sound good? Wouldn't it be great to have the boldness and the knowledge to speak for Christ at any given moment? It is possible, but it's not by our might or power. It's by the Lord's Spirit who lives within us. All of us are insufficient for witnessing, but He is strong. And He can be vital to us if we let Him.

"Whoever believes in the Son has eternal life, but whoever rejects the Son will not see life, for God's wrath remains on him."
John 3:36

We live in a mixed-up world with messed-up people who know little about God, Christ, and eternal life. We must recommit ourselves with compassion to reach all people for Christ. This is God's purpose for our lives, and this is your reason for participating in Walking In His Steps.

Notes From Reading:

____

____

____

Questions For The Group:

____

____

____

Prayer Request for Today:

____

____

____

About the Author

Dr. Pettigrew received his undergraduate degree at the University of Tennessee, his Master's degree at Murray State University, and his Doctoral degree from the University of Memphis.

Joe has been a high school teacher, university professor, College Dean, and the CEO for Leaderpoint Consulting Group. He has consulted with many of the most successful corporate leaders in the world and has close ties with many national Christian sports celebrities.

In 2008 he founded the national men's ministry, In The Zone. The ministry held in large arenas and churches was closed during Covid-19.

Joe has authored numerous books.

He has been married to Trudy for over 50 years, and together they have three children: Ashley, Tara, and Tyler. He also has seven grandchildren.

Thanks for reading Walking In His Steps.

For information about Joe speaking in your church or about ordering additional books, please contact info@inthezone.org.

May God Bless You.